D1488544

Foresight in Science

Forced into Service

Foresight in Science
Picking the Winners

John Irvine and Ben R. Martin

Frances Pinter (Publishers)
London and Dover, N.H.

© John Irvine and Ben R. Martin 1984

First published in Great Britain in 1984 by
Frances Pinter (Publishers) Limited
25 Floral Street, London WC2E 9DS

Published in the United States of America in 1984 by
Frances Pinter (Publishers), 51 Washington Street,
Dover, New Hampshire

British Library Cataloguing in Publication Data
Irvine, John
    Foresight in science.
    1. Science and state   2. Research
    I. Title   II. Martin, Ben R.
    507'.2   Q125
    ISBN 0–86187–496–X

Library of Congress Catalog Card No. 84–42926

Typeset by Joshua Associates, Oxford
Printed in Great Britain by SRP Ltd, Exeter

Contents

List of figures and tables

Preface and acknowledgements

This book is based on a report commissioned in Autumn 1983 on behalf of a Study Group of the Advisory Council for Applied Research and Development (ACARD) charged with undertaking a review of 'promising areas of science'. We are grateful to the Council for inviting us to carry out the study. However, this should not be taken to imply endorsement by the Council, officially or otherwise, of the data and findings contained in this book.

Support for writing up the study in book form was provided by the Leverhulme Trust. We should therefore like to record our sincere thanks to the Trust and to its Director, Dr Ronald Tress. Equally important, we must express our gratitude to a range of people without whose generous assistance the completion of this book would not have been possible. First, there are the 100 or so senior officials in government, industry, and research foundations, in France, Japan, the United States, and West Germany, who so freely gave up their time to be interviewed. While it would be invidious to single out individuals here, we would like to give special thanks to those who helped prepare and plan our schedule of visits during the fieldwork phase of the study. Among others, these include Dr Susan Cozzens of the National Science Foundation who helped set up our US interview programme, and the Science Attachés at the British Embassies in the four countries visited, in particular Dr C. Bradley and his staff in Tokyo.

We should also like to thank all those who have commented upon an earlier draft of this book, including many of the officials interviewed. Particularly thorough and helpful comments came from Dr Carlos Kruytbosch of the National Science Foundation, Mr Howard Gobstein of the US General Accounting Office, and Dr Kiyoshi Nagata of the Mitsubishi Research Institute.

In addition, a number of colleagues at the Science Policy Research Unit made major contributions during various phases of the study. We are especially grateful to both the Director of SPRU, Professor Geoffrey Oldham, and our programme-leader, Professor Keith Pavitt, for having encouraged us to undertake the study, and to Professor Linda Wilson, Mr Ian Miles and Dr Tom Whiston for providing a great deal of constructive and detailed suggestions for revision. While

acknowledging our considerable intellectual debt to all these individuals, we must nevertheless stress that ultimate responsibility for any
remaining errors or misinterpretations is ours alone.

Finally, we give deep-felt thanks to all those who have supported
us, both materially and emotionally, during the concentrated periods
in which most of this book was written. These include Mrs June
Mansbridge, our secretary, who did her best to organise our efforts
over this time and had to contend with assorted manuscripts of
varying degrees of illegibility, and our respective households, in
particular Valerie, Sarah and Paul Martin and William Bennett,
on the one side, and Dorothy Griffiths and Tariq and Polly, on the
other. To all, we again express our gratitude.

Ben Martin and John Irvine
Brighton, June 1984.

Foreword

How nations arrive at decisions relating to the support of research and development in science and technology is probably the major area of interest for the study of science policy. The extent of that support; the balance of funding between subjects with intrinsic or extrinsic merit; the degree of administrative *dirigisme*; the commitment to international collaboration in topics beyond, say, high-energy physics and space science—these and others are clearly crucial issues not only in relation to science and technology policy, but also to broader societal policies and objectives.

Three themes have apparently dominated the international R & D scene for at least a decade. The first is the recognition of the increasing pace of development in science and technology, a view which is now implanted at a political level—although not, perhaps, at as deep level of understanding as one might wish. The second is, relatedly, the articulation of a demand for relevance—for priority to be given to research having perceived socio-economic benefit. Thirdly, there is an understanding that resource limitations call for a degree of specialisation which should relate to strategic priorities.

Strategic research, the main concern of this book, is that research of a collateral nature required to achieve objectives which reflect both 'market pull' and 'science push' imperatives. That description may allow, in an iterative way, for the interactions, often perceived uncertainly, between opportunities flowing from scientific and technological advances and policy formulation; it carries a commitment to longer-term support than one necessarily envisages for applied research.

This review of support mechanisms in four leading industrial nations is of particular value following on, as it does, a review, for the UK Advisory Board for the Research Councils, of 'how provision should best be made for strategic research'. That review (Mason, 1983) made clear that the so-called customer–contractor relationship, largely constructed between Departments of State and three Research Councils, was not providing adequate support for important strategic research. Budgetary restraints were a major contribution to this problem but the customer–contractor relationships were flawed by the near-absence of significant scientific advice within some

Departments. It is obvious from the Irvine–Martin study that other countries have devised very different mechanisms for developing a consensus view on research programmes, and in particular on how to realise an integration of scientific, industrial and political requirements. One might also observe that Japan and the United States do appear to maintain programmes over the required time-scale much more consistently than their European counterparts; the latter have no insurmountable problems maintaining themselves in the front line of scientific advance but sustained investment in innovative technological programmes appears more difficult. It may be that initiatives like the UK and EEC programmes (Alvey and Esprit) on information technology will help to improve this situation.

It is a matter of judgement as to when resource limitations will require international collaboration in research areas which have traditionally been pursued on a national basis. Given their growing importance, it is perhaps surprising that there are not already more collaborative programmes in such areas as information technology and biotechnology. There is much discussion in the West on collaborative R & D programmes in defence but they often fail to emerge because of difficulties in reconciling operational requirements and timescales. In the civil sector, the ability to develop integrated R & D programmes in Europe, let alone between, say, Europe and Japan, is very limited. It is hoped that this book, by informing policy-makers of the institutional divergences within the developed world, will enable earlier and more rational planning not only of national research programmes but also collaborative programmes in high technology.

Sir Ronald Mason
1 July 1984

Reference

Mason, R. M. (1983), *A Study of Commissioned Research*, report prepared for the Advisory Board for the Research Councils, London, ABRC.

Foresight in Science

1 Introduction: the role of strategic research

1.1 Basic research in the new economic context

This book sets out to address one of the crucial problems currently facing policy-makers in both government and industry, that of picking 'winners' in basic science. To what extent is it possible to identify with any degree of confidence those areas of today's research that are likely to provide the knowledge-base for the important new technologies and industries of tomorrow? And what monitoring and forecasting techniques does past experience suggest are best suited to this task of identifying promising new areas of science?

The need to identify strategically important areas of basic research has emerged in the 1980s as a central concern in all the major industrial societies. While cutbacks in (or at least restrictions on the growth of) national science budgets have themselves led to new initiatives aimed at distributing more rationally and equitably the available funds (see, for example, the discussion in Irvine and Martin, 1984), it has been the increasing economic importance of a range of new 'basic technologies'[1] such as knowledge-engineering or information-technology, biological materials and processes, and micro-electronics that has propelled the issue of science policy squarely to the centre of public debate. This is reflected in the recent surge of publications concerned with science (as opposed to technology) policy (for example, Gibbons et al., 1984; Goldsmith, 1984; and Ronayne, 1984). It can also be seen in the importance accorded to basic research within national and international reports on science and technology in the 'new economic context' of the 1980s (for example, OECD, 1980; Panel on Advanced Technology Competition and the Industrialized Allies, 1983; and STA, 1982).[2]

At the heart of this new interest in research policy is the recognition that the emerging 'basic technologies' are all highly science-dependent, and that intellectual capital will play a far more important role in maintaining industrial competitiveness (at both company and national levels) than hitherto.[3] While it is certainly true that much of the scientific base of these technologies is already in place, the realisation of their potential for industrial application still depends on future developments in basic research. This has begun to result in new and qualitatively different demands being placed on the state-funded infrastructure for science. Not only has there been a growth in the demand by industry for highly trained recruits from the universities (with some countries already reporting significant shortages in software engineering and various applied biological and chemical specialties, for example), but the interface between academic research and industrial R & D has also assumed greater significance, as we shall see in later chapters. Many academic specialties funded primarily on a curiosity-orientated basis by national science foundations are now finding themselves drawn upon heavily by industry to help with their longer-term technological programmes.[4] Certain broad areas of 'pure' science are thus being transformed into what we shall term 'strategic research', and it is this process, together with the implications it has for the establishment of government R & D priorities, that forms the main subject of this book. Clearly, if early identification of promising areas of strategic research is possible, then targeted support by government can increase the likely future economic and technological benefits to industry—especially if effective knowledge-transfer mechanisms exist between academic institutions and industrial enterprises.

1.2 The concept of strategic research

At this stage, it is useful to clarify what is meant by the term 'strategic research', and to distinguish it from the more general category of 'basic research'. This is necessary since, as Mason (1983, pp. 13–14) points out, considerable confusion exists over the classification of research activities into 'basic', 'applied', 'strategic' and the like.

Perhaps the underlying reason behind this confusion is the fact that the classification employed in the 'Frascati Manual' (OECD, 1981), which sets out the internationally agreed categories for surveys of research and development (R & D), relies upon a threefold distinction between 'basic research', 'applied research' and 'experimental development'. Despite the undoubted value of this classificatory framework in helping achieve broadly comparable sets of cross-national R & D statistics, the categories have become less satisfactory over time as regards their operational utility. This is especially true for 'basic research', which can cover anything from what US R & D managers often will 'curiosity-oriented, proposal-driven research' carried out in universities, to longer-term work performed by mission-orientated government agencies, through to speculative industrial research where no specific application is yet in mind. The end result, not surprisingly, is a situation where different groups of scientists, different research organisations and agencies, and different types of industrial enterprise tend to use their own specialised classifications of research activity. Most academic researchers, for example, tend to refer to their work as 'pure' or 'fundamental' rather than as 'basic'.

The recent injection of the notion of 'strategic research' (which is not included among the 'Frascati' definitions) into debates about science policy has further broadened the range of terminological options available to describe basic research, particularly as little consensus exists over precisely what is meant by 'strategic research'. The difference between the following two definitions, both drawn from official British reports on science policy published in 1983, is readily apparent:

strategic research is used to denote collateral research required to achieve *national strategic objectives* that may originate from either of two directions (i) market pull, when a potential user has recognised that more background knowledge in a particular field is needed, and (ii) technology push, when research workers have recognised that a discovery may lead on to practical applications. [Mason, 1983, pp. 13–14, emphasis added.]

[Strategic research refers to] research in areas where *the basic principles are known*, but the final products have yet to be identified. [ACARD/ABRC, 1983, p. 11, emphasis added.]

For these reasons, it is clearly important to be precise about definitions. Figure 1.1 outlines the classification of R & D activities that is used in this book. It is based on a slight modification and extension of the 'Frascati' categories, and in our view presents a set of definitions more closely related to the actual R & D activities found in academia, government laboratories and industry.

As can be seen, the most important difference from the 'Frascati' classification is that the 'basic research' category has been subdivided into 'pure or curiosity-orientated research' and 'strategic research'. The former corresponds to the traditional notion of academic research carried out with the aim of producing new knowledge primarily for its own sake. By and large, finance for such research is obtained from national science foundations, with funding decisions being made on the basis of intrinsic scientific merit as perceived and judged by scientific peers (the so-called 'peer-review' system).

'Strategic research' differs most importantly from pure or curiosity-orientated research in the rationale behind its support, there being at least some expectation that it will contribute background knowledge required in the development of new technologies. Furthermore,

Nature of R & D		Main performer(s)
Basic Research: Original investigation with the primary aim of developing more complete knowledge or understanding of the subject(s) under study.	**Pure or curiosity-orientated research:**[a] Basic research carried out without working for long-term economic or social benefits other than the advancement of knowledge, and no positive efforts being made to apply the results to practical problems, or to transfer the results to sectors responsible for its application.	Normally (together with teaching) the main function of the academic university-based research system.
	Strategic research: Basic research carried out with the expectation that it will produce a broad base of knowledge likely to form the background to the solution of recognised current or future practical problems.	Carried out in universities and government laboratories, as well as in most larger science-based companies (in which it typically accounts for no more than 5–10 per cent of the R & D budget).
Applied or tactical research:[b] Original investigation undertaken in order to acquire new knowledge, and directed primarily towards specific practical aims or objectives such as determining possible uses for findings of basic research or solving already recognised problems.		Mainly carried out by industry and laboratories of mission-oriented government agencies, although also undertaken (under contract or as part of targeted government research programmes) within the academic research system.
Experimental development: Systematic work drawing on existing knowledge gained from research and/or practical experience that is directed towards producing new or improved materials, products, devices, services, systems or methods, including design and development of prototypes and processes.		Overwhelmingly carried out in industry (where it typically accounts for 80–90 per cent of company R & D budgets) and in mission-oriented government agencies (often where the state is also the customer for the final envisaged product, such as advanced military hardware).

Source: Derived from National Science Board (1983, p. 237), OECD (1981, pp. 25–36) and Ronayne (1984, p. 35).

[a] This is sometimes referred to as 'fundamental' research, although the term can also refer to certain longer-term elements of strategic research.

[b] This is also sometimes referred to as 'mission-oriented' research, particularly in US government agencies, although such work often incorporates shorter-term elements of strategic research.

Figure 1.1 Classificatory framework for R & D activities

it is by no means confined solely to the university laboratory. Large science-based firms, for example, typically choose to devote a limited (but probably increasing) proportion of their R & D budgets to those areas of basic research felt most likely to provide the new knowledge required to develop the products and processes of the future. Besides hoping to produce in-house at least one or two scientific 'winners', many firms use such research to develop links with the relevant academic research communities. Such links are generally essential if the firm is successfully to monitor and take advantage of the latest scientific results. They are also necessary to develop within the company the skills and techniques required to mount rapid R & D programmes on new research possibilities as and when they occur.

However, perhaps the greatest volume of strategic research is carried out by the state in its mission-orientated agencies, particularly those concerned with defence where significant basic research efforts are mounted in the scientific fields thought likely to provide the knowledge inputs to future weapon-systems. Such efforts will often be at the very forefront of science where the basic principles are *not* always known. The same is true for the strategic research carried out by universities, often under contract to industry or government agencies (defence agencies again figure prominently) or undertaken as part of a national or international initiative (such as the current EEC 'ESPRIT' programme on information technology). In many respects, the actual *content* of such work will be little different from that of academic research funded on a 'pure' or 'curiosity-orientated' basis.

Finally, we should note that the remaining two categories of 'applied or tactical research' and 'experimental development' differ only in minor respects from those used in the 'Frascati Manual'. Such R & D is in large part carried out in industry and in mission-orientated government agencies. Although also an important subject of concern in science and technology policy, the techniques used to pick future 'winners' in applied research differ markedly from those in basic research where there is a much wider range of uncertainty. Important though it is, applied research is not, however, a main theme of this book.

1.3 Strategic research as a policy concern

Disagreement over 'strategic research' has by no means been confined to discussion of semantics. To a very real extent, it also represents the onset of a fundamental debate over the rationale for state-funding of basic science. On one side, certain sections of the academic community (particularly those in areas of 'pure' research generously supported in the past) argue that the application of criteria other than internal 'scientific' ones to prioritise certain fields at the expense of others is a dangerous new development that is to be resisted at all costs.[5] Others, however, not only in industry and government but also in national science foundations,[6] are increasingly arguing that external criteria should be employed in decisions relating to areas of basic research with some strategic significance. For example, many of the industrial R & D managers interviewed in the study we shall be describing advocated greater use of long-term technological and economic criteria (along with the usual scientific ones) to determine the distribution of public funds between broad fields of basic research, although they were apparently content to leave lower-level decisions on the allocation of resources between different programmes and projects to the scientific community and traditional peer-review mechanisms. If anything, the concern of such industrialists was that academic 'pure' research was not sufficiently strong, and that inadequacies and inefficiencies in the peer-review system may have given rise to uneven standards within academic science, as well as hindering the prompt reallocation of funds from declining research specialties to those identified on the basis of internal scientific criteria as having intellectual promise for the future. Much curiosity-orientated research is intrinsically unpredictable, and industrial research managers appreciate only too well that over-elaborate attempts to forecast 'winners' are likely to prove counter-productive. As with applied research, pure or curiosity-orientated research *per se* will not be a major theme in our subsequent discussions.

Instead, we shall concentrate on two central issues that need to be addressed by governments in determining policies for the support of strategic research. The first concerns the extent to which it is possible to exercise foresight in relation to strategic research. Can one identify those areas of curiosity-orientated research in the process of being transformed into 'strategic' areas, i.e. that are beginning to show promise of constituting a knowledge base that, with further funding, might eventually contribute to the solution of important practical problems? Among the policy questions that this raises are the following:

(a) What monitoring and forecasting techniques can be used to ensure that government and research-funding agencies immediately become aware of promising areas of science as they emerge?

(b) What mechanisms might help industry to recognise promptly the potential of new 'science-push' opportunities?

(c) What procedures would enable those in universities and government research institutes to recognise the potential value of their latest work by rendering them more aware of the basic technological programmes underway in related science-based industrial sectors and the associated plans for new lines of product and process development?

In what follows, we shall use the term 'foresight activities' as a form of short-hand to describe the techniques, mechanisms and procedures for attempting to identify areas of basic research beginning to exhibit strategic potential.

The second major issue relates to the role of government in providing direct infrastructural research support for industry. In line with the increased research intensity of many industrial sectors, there has, as noted earlier, been a growing recognition among science-based firms of the need to develop at an early stage an in-house capacity in those areas of research likely to be central to their future. However, strategic research is inherently risky and often expensive. Moreover, investment in such research may not yield dividends that are sufficiently immediate or firm-specific for the work to warrant priority over other apparently more pressing types of R & D. As a result, recent years have seen a trend in government strategies for the support of R & D away from providing subsidies for applied research and development and towards funding more basic research. As is reported in later chapters, this trend has been particularly pronounced not only in the United States and West Germany but also in Japan. It can be seen as part of a general move towards government support for collective research (cf. Rothwell and Zegveld, 1981). Governments are now recognising the need to concentrate more funds on providing comprehensive infrastructural support for longer-term strategic research, as is clear from the following statement: '[strategic research] is often outside the funding capabilities of individual firms: in such situations, collective action—perhaps with Government assistance—is required.' (ACARD/ABRC, 1983, p. 11.)

Since funds for supporting strategic industrial research will, like those for curiosity-orientated and strategic academic research, always be limited, choices have to be made as to *which* areas among the many possible options merit state support. The principal criterion underlying such a choice should surely be, 'Which research areas are likely to lead to the greatest economic and social benefits?' If so, then some attempt must be made by government to evaluate the likely technological and commercial impacts of the different areas of research identified as strategic by industry, and to ensure that adequate mechanisms exist to identify and support promising new areas of research under study in university and government laboratories.

1.4 Origins and structure of the book

It was concern with such issues that led the British Advisory Council for Applied Research and Development (ACARD) to set up a study group in Autumn 1983 to survey current scientific developments and identify work with commercial and economic promise for the medium- to long-term future. To provide one of the inputs into this study, the Science Policy Research Unit (SPRU) was commissioned to undertake a small project with the following objectives:

(a) to analyse attempts made in France, West Germany, Japan and the United States over the last twenty years to identify emerging areas of strategic research that at the time showed long-term promise[7] of leading to significant commercial benefits;
(b) to examine the role, if any, that these forecasts played in promoting such developments;
(c) to evaluate restrospective studies tracing back the scientific origins of significant technological innovations in order to determine whether the subsequent economic impact of the preceding research could have been predicted.

On the basis of the results obtained, SPRU would then offer suggestions as to approaches ACARD might adopt in its own survey of promising scientific areas.

This book represents a revised and extended version of our report to ACARD (Irvine and Martin, 1983). In some chapters, despite significant reworking, our coverage of the available material is still less comprehensive and some of the arguments put forward less well documented than we would have ideally liked. This stems from the fact that the original study had to be completed in three months. However, because the report brought together a great deal of contemporary material on a subject that is of current concern, we decided to publish immediately rather than take the additional time required to produced a more polished 'academic' version.

The information we drew upon came from two main sources:

(a) a review of the literature on scientific and technological forecasting and on science and technology policy, including relevant government reports; and

(b) in-depth interviews carried out with some hundred senior officials in government, industry and research foundations in France, West Germany, Japan and the United States.

Among the published material surveyed were:

(a) various individual forecasting exercises and retrospective analyses of the historical links between curiosity-orientated research, strategic research, applied R & D and innovation;
(b) the research literature on the strengths and weaknesses of different techniques for scientific and technological forecasting;
(c) general reports on science and technology policy-making in the four countries visited, in particular documents relating to the use of research forecasts.

In total, around forty organisations were visited. These can be divided into five categories:

(a) government ministries and departments—the French Ministry of Industry and Research (MIR); the West German Federal Ministry for Research and Technology (BMFT); the Japanese Ministry of Education, Science and Culture (Monbusho), Ministry of International Trade and Industry (MITI), Science and Technology Agency (STA) and Council for Science and Technology; and the US Department of Energy (DoE), General Accounting Office (GAO), Office of Management and Budget (OMB), and Office of Science and Technology Policy of the President (OSTP);
(b) national research-funding agencies the French Centre Nationale de la Recherche Scientifique (CNRS); the Deutsche Forschungsgemeinschaft (DFG), Fraunhofer-Gesellschaft (FhG), and Max-Planck-Gesellschaft (MPG) in West Germany; and the US National Science Foundation (NSF);
(c) large science-based firms covering a range of industries currently witnessing major technological change, and including some of the world-leaders in their sectors;
(d) technical consultancy organisations—the Center for Research Planning (CRP), Computer Horizons Incorporated (CHI Research), the Institute for the Future and SRI International in the US; and in Japan the Mitsubishi Research Institute, the National Institute for Research Advancement and the Nomura Research Institute;
(e) other relevant organisations—the Long-Term Credit Bank of Japan; the US National Academy of Sciences (NAS); and the Directorate for Science, Technology, and Industry (DSTI) of

the Organisation for Economic Co-operation and Development (OECD).

Interviews typically lasted up to two hours, and were usually carried out using a structured questionnaire. Among the questions asked were the following:

(a) To what extent has the organisation previously attempted to undertake longer-term forecasting of the likely economic impact of more basic scientific and technological research? What was the rationale behind such forecasts, and who was responsible for them?

(b) What has been the experience with forecasting? In retrospect, how successful or useful have the forecasts proved?

(c) What forecasting methods have been used? Have these been of a quantitative nature (for example, trend-extrapolation), or have more qualitative approaches such as Delphi techniques been employed? How has the approach changed over time, and what were the reasons behind any change?

(d) In relation to individual forecasting exercises, what were the reasons for undertaking the study? Was it carried out internally or by outside consultants? What time-horizon and forecasting methods were used? What was the relative emphasis given to science and technology 'push', to market 'pull' and to the infrastructural factors which often play a crucial part in the growth and commercialisation of promising new areas of science? What were the main conclusions, and what attempts were made to validate them? How were the results used, especially in restructuring expenditure on longer-term strategic research? With hindsight, how accurate were the predictions, and what were the successes and failures of the study?

(e) In general terms, how valuable have government forecasts of the commercial prospects for long-term strategic research proved? Is there a role for government in such matters, or should forecasting be left to industry and commercial consultancy organisations?

The structure of this book in large part reflects the tasks set by ACARD for its commissioned study. In the next chapter, we report the results of our review of retrospective studies of the scientific origins of significant technological innovations, drawing a number of lessons of relevance to the prospects for longer-term research forecasting. The following four chapters (Chapters 3 to 6) then consider, in turn, experiences with scientific and technological forecasting in France, West Germany, the United States and Japan, noting the strengths and weaknesses of the different approaches adopted by government, national research-funding agencies, firms and consultancy organisations, and commenting upon the accuracy of the various predictions and their subsequent impact on research policy. Next, Chapter 7 summarises and contrasts the lessons that can be learned from past experience in the four countries, arriving at a number of tentative conclusions about how (and how not) to evaluate the prospects for promising areas of science. Finally, Chapter 8 presents some necessarily personal views on what we feel to be the most promising approaches to picking future scientific 'winners'. It will not take the reader long to recognise the profound impact that our visit to Japan had on our views about how to identify 'winners' in strategic research, and much of what we say refers to what the Western industrial nations can learn from their technologically advanced Asian competitor.

NOTES

1. We use here the Japanese term for what is sometimes known as 'generic' technology, i.e. fields of technological research (often newly emerging) with applications across a range of industrial sectors and product-lines (see, for example, Moritani, 1983).
2. It is interesting to note that scientific and technological concerns have for the first time begun to appear as major items on the agenda at Western inter-governmental meetings such as the Versailles Summit. The activities of bodies such as the NATO Science Committee have also started to achieve greater prominence.
3. The Japanese in particular have identified the need to improve 'creativity' as one of the main science-policy goals of the 1980s (see STA, 1982).
4. In the chemicals and allied sector, for example, most of the citations (65 per cent) made to prior research in a survey of recent US patent applications were to publications in essentially basic science journals. This compared with 24 per cent to applied science, 7 per cent to engineering science and 4 per cent to applied technology journals (Carpenter, 1983, p. 22).
5. For example, the introduction to a recent US report ended with the following ringing denunciation: 'These are difficult times, and the remainder of this decade may be an era of economic stresses. The temptation is to select, to have priorities, to mark some scientific fields as critical to the nation's welfare and others less so. There is no specific historical experience to support this. If one lesson has been learned in all of the studies of the relation of scientific knowledge to technological advancement and in turn to economic strengths, it is that we will be surprised. We cannot choose selective excellence in science.' (Bloom, 1983, p. 13.)
6. One noteworthy example in Britain concerns the Science Board of the

Science and Engineering Research Council (SERC). A recent report of the Board (which is headed by Professor J. Cadogan, R & D Director at British Petroleum) assessed the relative levels of support given to the broad fields of academic science. Coining the term 'core areas of science', the report departed from previous policy in concluding that 'it is important to recognise that research in these themes is crucial in underpinning the science-based sectors of the national economy. Although it is not the Science Board's job or intent to support research specifically for industry, it believes that it must support core science in such a way that British industry prospers'. (SERC, 1984, p. 7.) It remains to be seen whether this recognition of the need to use strategic criteria to determine, at least in part, the relative levels of support to broad fields of research activity will actually be implemented by SERC in its future funding policies.

7. 'Long-term' is defined here as ten years or more into the future. Similarly, we shall use 'medium-term' to denote a time-horizon of approximately five years, while 'short-term' refers to the next one or two years.

REFERENCES

ACARD/ABRC (1983), *First Joint Report by the Chairmen of the Advisory Council for Applied Research and Development (ACARD) and the Advisory Board for the Research Councils (ABRC)*, London, HMSO, Cmnd. 8957.

Bloom, F. E. (1983), 'Science, technology, and the national agenda', introduction to *Frontiers in Science and Technology: A Selected Outlook*, a report by the Committee on Science, Engineering, and Public Policy, New York, W. H. Freeman.

Carpenter, M. P. (1983), 'Patent citations as indicators of scientific and technological linkages', paper presented at AAAS Annual Meeting, Detroit, Michigan, 30 May, mimeo, Cherry Hill, N.J., CHI Research.

Gibbons, M., Gummett, P. and Udgaonkar, B. M. (eds) (1984), *Science and Technology Policy in the 1980s and Beyond*, London, Longman.

Goldsmith, M. (ed.) (1984), *UK Science Policy: A Critical Review of Policies for Publicly Funded Research*, London, Longman.

Irvine, J. and Martin, B. R. (1983), *Project Foresight: An Assessment of Approaches to Identifying Promising New Areas of Science*, unpublished report prepared for the Advisory Council for Applied Research and Development by the Science Policy Research Unit, University of Sussex, Brighton.

Irvine, J. and Martin, B. R. (1984), 'What direction for basic scientific research?', in M. Gibbons *et al.* (eds) (1984), pp. 67–98.

Mason, R. M. (1983), *A Study of Commissioned Research*, report prepared for the Advisory Board for the Research Councils, London, ABRC.

Moritani, M. (1983), *Advanced Technology and the Japanese Contribution*, Tokyo, Nomura Securities Company Ltd.

National Science Board (1983), *Science Indicators 1982*, Washington, D.C., NSB/NSF.

OECD (1980), *Technical Change and Economic Policy: Science and Technology in the New Economic Context*, Paris, OECD.

OECD (1981), *The Measurement of Scientific and Technical Activities* ('Frascati Manual' 1980), Paris, OECD.

Panel on Advanced Technology Competition and the Industrialized Allies (1983), *International Competition in Advanced Technology: Decisions for America*, Washington, D.C., National Academy Press.

Ronayne, J. (1984), *Science in Government*, London, Edward Arnold.

Rothwell, R. and Zegveld, W. (1981), *Industrial Innovation and Public Policy: Preparing for the 1980s and the 1990s*, London, Frances Pinter.

SERC (1984), *A Strategy for the Support of Core Science*, report of the Science Board of the Science and Engineering Research Council, Swindon, SERC.

STA (1982), *White Paper on Science and Technology 1982*, Tokyo, Science and Technology Agency (in Japanese). A full English language translation can be found in *Japan Science and Technology Outlook*, Tokyo, Fuji Corporation, 1983.

2 Learning from history: retrospective studies of innovation

2.1 Science, technology and the innovation process

Over the last twenty years, a number of important studies have been undertaken concerning the research origins of major technological innovations, and assessing the extent to which basic science has contributed to their development. In this chapter, we evaluate some of the more influential of these studies to ascertain what light, if any, they shed on the problem of identifying emerging areas of strategic research.

First, however, a brief historical digression is necessary to consider the nature of technological innovation. It was the Second World War and such technological developments as the atomic bomb which demonstrated, to many for the first time, what could be achieved by harnessing the efforts of scientists within R & D programmes orientated to meeting national goals. In the case of the bomb, the research that made it possible—namely, the work on splitting the atom—had, at the time it was carried out, no apparent practical application. This example, perhaps above all others, helped establish the still strongly held notion that technological innovation is 'driven' by advances in curiosity-orientated science. Such a view was most clearly expounded in a politically influential book by the prominent American scientist, Dr Vannevar Bush (1945), entitled *Science, The Endless Frontier*: 'New products and processes are founded on new principles and conceptions which, in turn, are developed by research in the purest realms of science.' (p. 19.)

This view, which was to hold sway for the next two decades, is now generally termed the 'science-push' model of innovation. It can be depicted as follows:

Curiosity-orientated $\longrightarrow$ Applied $\longrightarrow$ Experimental $\longrightarrow$ Innovation
research   research   development

One reason why such a theory of innovation was particularly appealing to basic scientists was that it provided a ready argument to support their claims in the post-war years for substantially increased public funding.

In the 1960s, however, an alternative model of innovation began to attract support, particularly among economists. According to this model, innovations are 'called forth' by new or changed market demands, as illustrated below:

Market $\longrightarrow$ Applied $\longrightarrow$ Experimental $\longrightarrow$ Innovation
demand   research   development

Since this 'demand-pull' model of innovation clearly has very different policy implications from the 'science-push' version (in particular, with regard to the degree that the state should intervene to support basic research), science-policy researchers during the 1960s and early 1970s devoted considerable effort in attempting to ascertain which of the two competing models most accurately characterises the innovation process. What emerged from the resulting empirical studies was that most innovations in practice fit neither of these simple models. In other words, the innovation process cannot generally be represented as a linear sequence of events with a single cause—successful innovations depend not only on coupling a new market demand to a new technological opportunity, but also on a multitude of other factors interrelated in a complex manner. The implications of this finding for our concern with identifying important new areas of strategic research are explored later in this chapter.

2.2 Project Hindsight

The first major retrospective study that we shall review, Project Hindsight, was undertaken in the mid-1960s by the United States Department of Defense (DoD). The study assessed the relative contributions of science and technology to the development of twenty weapon-systems (including the Polaris missile, the Minuteman ICBM, and the C–141 aircraft). It was undertaken by DoD scientists and engineers, and involved a total of over fifty person-years of effort.[1] The project team attempted to identify the factors underlying successful R & D programmes, with the aim of improving DoD resource-allocation and programme-management procedures. Among the issues considered were the optimum balance between basic and applied research, and whether R & D was carried out more effectively by DoD laboratories, industry, or universities. An attempt was also made to measure that part of the increase in cost-effectiveness of new weapon-systems over previous generation systems attributable to DoD investment in R & D.

The approach adopted involved groups of between five and ten scientists and engineers dissecting the various weapon-systems into their constituent components. These were then examined to assess the relative contributions made by science and technology in increasing the performance (or the cost-effectivness) of the new weapon-systems over their predecessors. Each discrete contribution was termed an 'event'; they were classified as either 'science events' if they stemmed from pure or strategic research (the terms 'undirected science' and 'directed science' were actually used), or 'technology events' if they arose from mission-oriented R & D and resulted in a new or improved technique, material, component or subsystem. Analysis of the twenty weapon-systems yielded nearly 700 distinct research and exploratory development events, only 8 per cent of which were found to be 'science events' compared with 92 per cent 'technology events'. Furthermore, nearly 80 per cent of those 'science events' were the result of research orientated toward a DoD need, while most of the remainder stemmed from research with a commercial objective; only around 4 per cent were the fruit of pure or 'curiosity-oriented' research. As regards their source, 39 per cent of all events resulted from in-house R & D in a DoD laboratory, 49 per cent were the product of industrial research, and a mere 9 per cent arose from the university sector. (Of the remaining 3 per cent, two-thirds were contributed by non-DoD federal laboratories, and one-third by foreign laboratories.) Thus, basic research had apparently been relatively unimportant in the development of the weapon-systems examined. The most successful R & D, it seemed, was that orientated to specific DoD requirements (a clear understanding of a DoD need underpinned 95 per cent of all events). The pay-back from such R & D was found to be considerably greater than the investment, and of an order of magnitude higher than the benefits generated by a similar level of investment in research *not* specifically addressed to defence needs (cf. Sherwin and Isenson, 1966, pp. 11–15).

Almost inevitably, Project Hindsight had a considerable and immediate impact, not only with respect to its implications for defence R & D expenditure, but also because of the doubt it cast on the conventional wisdom that generous investment in basic science was a prerequisite for maintaining US supremacy in advanced technology. However, the study was open to at least two major criticisms. First, an arbitrary cut-off of twenty years was used in tracing back the science and technology events, thereby excluding from consideration any significant basic research arising before this time and inevitably reducing the apparent relative importance of basic research. Secondly, the fact that the twenty weapon-systems chosen for study had been selected by DoD staff inevitably created a suspicion among some that the sample was biased in order to provide support for those arguing in favour of increased funding for in-house applied research.

2.3 TRACES

Given the policy implications of the Project Hindsight findings, it is not surprising that the US academic science community was among the first and most vociferous critics of the interim report when it appeared in 1966. The National Science Foundation was far from convinced of the validity of the claimed results and very soon thereafter invited proposals for a 'study to investigate the manner in which non-mission-related research has contributed over a number of years to practical innovations of economic or social importance' (quoted in Ronayne, 1984, p. 56). In 1967, the Illinois Institute of Technology was commissioned to carry out the study. The report from the Illinois team (IIT Research Institute, 1968), which was completed at the end of 1968, was entitled 'Technology in Retrospect and Critical Events in Science', and gave rise to the acronym, TRACES, by which the work came to be known.

    TRACES adopted a similar approach to that used in Project Hindsight, involving the tracing of critical research events leading up to five major technological innovations (magnetic ferrites, the video tape-recorder, the oral contraceptive pill, the electron microscope and matrix isolation), but in this case the historical cut-off selected was fifty rather than twenty years. The research traces of one of the most interesting innovations—the video tape-recorder—are given in Figure 2.1. This reveals how the development of this particular innovation depended on the merging of several streams of scientific and technological activity, including control theory, magnetic and recording materials, magnetic theory, magnetic recording, electronics and frequency modulation. Similarly, to take another example (not illustrated), it was the combination of research in the fields of hormones, steroid chemistry and the physiology of reproduction that eventually led to the development of the oral contraceptive pill in the 1950s.

    The research events identified by the Illinois team were classified into three categories according to whether they arose from (i)

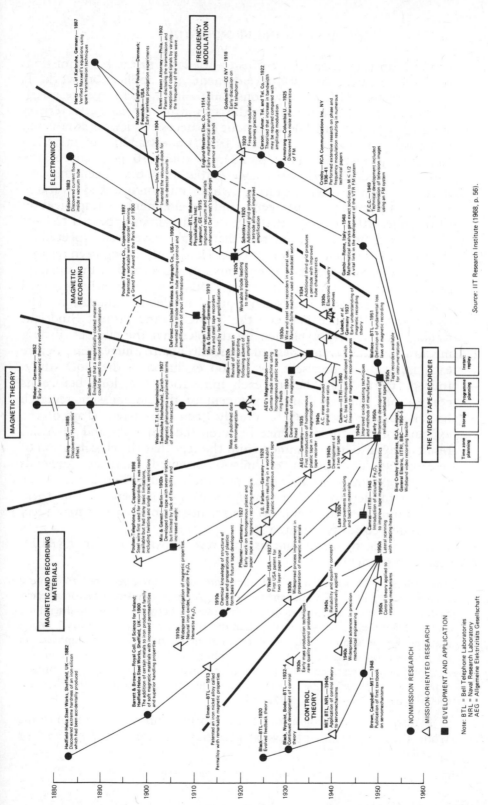

Figure 2.1 The research origins of the video tape-recorder

Source: IIT Research Institute (1968, p. 56).

non-mission (i.e. essentially curiosity-oriented) research, (ii) mission-oriented research, or (iii) development and application work. It was found that all five innovations had their origins in basic research. For example, the tracings of the evolution of magnetic ferrites revealed that 'the early development of successful devices stimulated non-mission research to achieve a basic understanding of materials and their properties' (ibid., p. 23). In total, 70 per cent of the 340 identified research events were found to have been the product of non-mission research, while mission-oriented research accounted for only 20 per cent, and development and application work under 10 per cent. Furthermore, universities appeared to have played a far more important role than might have been expected on the basis of the findings from Project Hindsight, having been responsible for three-quarters of the non-mission and a third of the mission-oriented research events. In short, TRACES apparently provided evidence to support the 'science-push' model of innovation. The significant difference between the TRACES and Project Hindsight findings was largely explained by the fact that the number of non-mission research events peaked some twenty to thirty years before each innovation, precisely the period excluded in the DoD study. Indeed, thirty years before each innovation (i.e. long before its conception), no less than 45 per cent of the non-mission research had, according to TRACES, already been completed. (Part of the explanation for the difference between the Hindsight and TRACES results may also have stemmed from the fact that the classification of research as 'non-mission' or 'mission-oriented' inevitably depends to some extent on who carried out the classification. Some of the research funded by US mission agencies may be perceived by them as 'mission-oriented', while to the scientists concerned it may seem essentially 'curiosity-oriented'.)

A number of other conclusions were drawn from the TRACES study. In particular,

The diversity of knowledge, and therefore of research required to achieve innovation, . . . [is] an important factor . . . Another important factor inherent in several of the tracings was that of interaction between scientific disciplines and/or highly effective personal communication. . . . [Consequently,] organizations which support and guide research must increase their emphasis on communication particularly among disciplines and between non-mission and mission-oriented research. . . . The continued involvement of a variety of institutions would appear to be a worthwhile objective to help meet the need for diversity of research. [ibid., pp. 22–3.]

It was this clear recognition that important innovations often result from the interaction of several previously unconnected streams of scientific and technological activity that remains perhaps the most important finding from TRACES, a point to which we return later.

2.4 Interactions of science and technology in the innovation process

While TRACES provided NSF and the US science community with evidence to defend basic research (cf. Walsh, 1973, p. 847), its findings also soon became the subject of considerable criticism, in particular on the grounds that the sample of five innovations studied was not entirely representative. Partly to assuage such doubts, NSF commissioned from Battelle Laboratories a more sophisticated version of TRACES. Completed in 1973 at a cost of $250,000, the Battelle study traced the main research and development events leading up to eight major innovations (the heart pacemaker, the hybrid grains associated with the 'green revolution', electrophotography, input–output analysis, organophosphorus insecticides and, for comparative purposes, three of the innovations previously considered in TRACES). Where the new study differed from its predecessor was in pinpointing from among the large number of research and development events the few *decisive* events without which the innovation would not have occurred. When these were analysed, it was discovered that 15 per cent were associated with non-mission research, 45 per cent with mission-oriented research, and 39 per cent with development work—a result much closer in line with Project Hindsight than TRACES. (It is significant that decisive events were often found to arise at the convergence of previously separate streams of research activity.) However, the corresponding figures for *all* research and development events, decisive or otherwise, were 34 per cent, 38 per cent, and 26 per cent (Battelle, 1973, p. 4.8)—that is, intermediate between Project Hindsight and TRACES.

In addition, the Battelle study went on to ask, 'Can innovation be managed?' Analysis of the eight traces revealed over twenty factors determining the direction and rate of the innovation process. In particular, 'recognition of a technical opportunity' and 'recognition of a need' were both identified as key factors in most decisive events (in 87 per cent and 69 per cent of cases respectively). Also important were good 'internal R & D management' (present in 66 per cent of decisive events) and the existence of a 'technical entrepreneur' (56 per cent) (ibid., p. 4.6). This latter finding gave rise to the comment that, 'If any suggestion were to be made as to what should be done to promote innovation, it would be to find—

if one can!—technical entrepreneurs' (quoted in Walsh, 1973, p. 846).

2.5 Study of biomedical science by Comroe and Dripps

One intrinsic problem common to Hindsight, TRACES, and the Battelle report is that all were based on a case-history approach, creating doubts as to whether the procedure for selecting the innovations studied had been free from bias. In an attempt to obtain more systematic statistical evidence on the relative contribution of basic research, Comroe and Dripps (1976, pp. 105–11) focused on an entire field—clinical advances in treating cardiovascular and pulmonary diseases. The procedure adopted involved (i) requesting forty physicians to identify the most important clinical advances in the field since 1940; (ii) analysing these advances in order to draw up two lists, one for pulmonary and one for cardiovascular advances; (iii) sending the lists to over forty specialists in each field who voted on the relative importance of the various advances; (iv) preparing a short-list of the top ten most significant clinical advances; (v) drawing upon the advice of 140 consultants to establish which areas of basic research had contributed to each advance, thereby identifying 137 bodies of essential scientific knowledge; (vi) scanning 4,000 relevant research publications and selecting 2,500 which particularly advanced the 137 essential bodies of knowledge; (vii) using consultants to narrow the list to approximately 500 key articles; and (viii) dividing the 500 articles into 'clinically-oriented' papers and 'others' (essentially curiosity-oriented research unrelated to any specific biomedical problem).

Overall, Comroe and Dripps found that 41 per cent of the key articles were non-clinically oriented. From this, they concluded that,

planning for future clinical advances must include generous support for innovative and imaginative research that bears no discernible relation to a clinical problem at the time of peer-review . . .; basic research, as we have defined it, pays off in terms of key discoveries almost twice as handsomely as other types of research and development combined. [Comroe and Dripps, 1976, pp. 109–11.]

They did not, however, address the crucial question of whether one can identify in a general way the areas of basic research most likely to yield clinical advances.

2.6 Other retrospective studies

Among the numerous other restrospective studies undertaken over the last two decades which have explored the interface between basic research and technological innovation,[2] four in particular merit brief discussion.

The first is the analysis by Myers and Marquis (1969) of 567 innovations in five industrial sectors (railways, railway-equipment, building-materials, computers and computer peripherals). Executive and technical personnel were interviewed in a cross-section of firms in the five sectors to establish which factors had been most important in stimulating each innovation. Myers and Marquis found that advances in basic research were the most important contributory factor in 21 per cent of cases, while market factors were predominant in 45 per cent, and manufacturing technology factors in 30 per cent. From this, it was concluded that 'three-fourths of the innovations could be classed as responses to demand recognition' (ibid., p. 31).

An equally complex picture of the role of basic research in innovation emerged from the second study by a group at Manchester University (Langrish *et al.*, 1972). This focused on UK firms that had received the Queen's Award to Industry. In 1966 and 1967, sixty-six such awards were made involving eighty-four technological innovations. Distinguishing between the two models of innovation discussed in section 2.1, the Manchester researchers found that, while very few of the innovations fitted either model perfectly, it was clear that none could be described as having been 'pushed' by a scientific discovery and only five had been initiated by a technological discovery. In short, basic research had apparently played a very minor role in the innovations studied.

A different approach was adopted by the Science Policy Research Unit in the third study, which examined twenty-nine matched pairs (subsequently increased to forty-three) of commercially successful and unsuccessful innovations in the chemicals and scientific-instruments sectors (SPRU, 1972). Project SAPPHO (Scientific Activity Predictor from Patterns with Heuristic Origins) was unique in that it analysed the factors retarding or preventing innovation. Although it did not specifically assess the contributions made by basic science relative to more applied R & D, one interesting result that did emerge was that, while half the firms studied were undertaking a certain amount of more basic research, there was only a modest correlation between this factor and successful innovation. On the other hand, it was found that 'successful innovators

make more effective use of outside technology and scientific advice'
(ibid., p. 5).

In the final retrospective study to be considered here, Gibbons
and Johnston (1972, and 1974) analysed the information inputs
required to solve the technical problems encountered in the R & D
leading up to thirty innovations. Unlike in other studies, these
inputs were classified as 'scientific' or 'technical' according to the
source rather than the content of the information. While only
a small fraction (about 20 per cent) of all the information utilised
in the innovations examined was scientific in character, it was
found that the information most useful in solving technical problems
had been drawn from scientific journals, while personal contacts
with outside scientists had also proved valuable. The overall conclusion of Gibbons and Johnston, and one which can be drawn from
all the studies surveyed here, is that 'the relationship between science
and industrial technology is more complex than previously assumed
by either scientists or economists; there exists a wide variety of
potential forms of interaction' (ibid., p. 241).

2.7 Lessons from retrospective studies of innovation

While the picture that emerges from retrospective studies of innovation is exceedingly complex, one conclusion that stands out clearly
is that neither the 'science-push' nor the 'demand-pull' model provides
an adequate description of the innovation process. Paradoxically,
it is this negative result which ensures that there is a role for longer-
term research forecasting. If innovations were driven simply by
advances in curiosity-orientated research, then forecasting would
be virtually impossible because such advances are generally unpredictable in nature. On the other hand, if innovations were merely
called forth by changed market demands, then research forecasting
would be reduced to little more than long-range market prediction.
It is precisely because innovations tend to require both advances in
scientific understanding and changes in market demand that the
concept of strategic research forecasting becomes meaningful.

Furthermore, the fact that the above studies demonstrate the
existence of certain links, albeit rather complex ones, between
curiosity-orientated research and subsequent technological innovation lends credence to the conventional wisdom that modern industrial states need to support a balanced portfolio of basic-research
activities. However, given that the resources available are finite, some
selection is clearly inevitable. The question, therefore, is whether
any lessons can be drawn from retrospective studies in relation to

identifying *which* lines of research are likely to be of greatest economic significance.

A number of related observations need to be made. First, most retrospective studies have focused on individual *radical* innovations where the innovator has synthesised a set of technical possibilities to produce a commercially (or militarily) significant new product or process. It is evident from the Battelle, TRACES and Comroe and Dripps studies that individual lines of research evolve in a complex fashion, and that serendipity plays a major role—particularly in the earlier and more basic phases (see Figure 2.1). As a result, monitoring vast numbers of active lines of basic research cannot realistically be proposed as a tool for predicting specific radical innovations. Indeed, the key research events which precede such innovations can often only be identified with the benefit of hindsight. Radical innovations stemming from more curiosity-orientated research are probably not, therefore, an appropriate subject for longer-term foresight activities.

However, what can certainly be recognised, and to a certain extent even be predicted, is the *synthesis* or confluence of previously distinct lines of research that often makes an innovation possible. Project Hindsight, for example, noted in connection with this phenomenon that 'it is the *synergistic effect* of these many [R & D] events which is the primary source of the increase in performance or the reduction in procurement cost compared to its predecessor' (Sherwin and Isenson, 1966, p. 4, emphasis added).

The importance of confluence emerged even more clearly from the Battelle study:

The occurrence of an unplanned confluence of technology was characteristic of six of the innovations. Interestingly enough, confluence of technology occurred for the other four innovations as well, but *as a result of deliberate planning*, rather than by accident. In . . . [one] innovation, organophosphorus insecticides, a planned interdisciplinary team was organized from the outset of the innovative process. [Battelle, 1973, p. 3.2, emphasis added.]

The obvious conclusion, and the one which the Battelle study went on to draw, is that '[because] confluence of technology . . . is essential to innovation, . . . it presents an opportunity for management, by promoting interdisciplinary R & D teams, to accelerate the innovative process' (ibid., p. 3.4).

While, as we have seen, the prospects for forecasting in relation to radical innovation are rather limited, the same is not true for *incremental* innovation. A strong national capability in incremental innovation is probably as important as the capacity to innovate radically. One reason (in addition to those discussed previously) why Project Hindsight arrived at very different conclusions from TRACES is that it focused on large-scale but essentially incremental military innovations, drawing primarily upon strategic rather than curiosity-orientated research. Though still a difficult task, it is considerably simpler to foresee the areas of strategic research on which the next-generation of weapon-systems will be based. The same is true in many other science-based industries, where (as we shall see later) the most successful firms already tend to be reasonably aware of those areas of strategic research likely to be drawn upon in their future R & D. Indeed, one task of corporate R & D departments is to monitor external scientific activity so that such predictions can be made.

The crucial lesson from retrospective analyses, therefore, is that by far the best prospects for forecasting exist in relation to strategic rather than curiosity-orientated research. Hence, the goal of government must be to develop procedures for recognising promptly when curiosity-orientated research is evolving into an area with important strategic prospects,[3] and then to mobilise resources to give priority to such areas. Governments face a growing obligation to provide infrastructural support for new and more sophisticated science-based industry—especially skilled research staff to work on the next generation of technologies, and funds for risky, pre-competitive strategic research that is most effectively carried out collectively. The difficulty lies in developing appropriate mechanisms to monitor research developments across all sectors (without which priority-setting is clearly impossible), while avoiding the dangers often associated with central planning (for example, excessive bureaucracy).

One obvious way for government to proceed (and one considered later in our discussion of Japan) is to exploit the monitoring activities already carried out by industry, 'tapping into' the forecasting and prioritisation procedures of major R & D-based firms. The role of government is thus confined to synthesising from such work a set of broader forecasts for the main industrial sectors. By combining this with suitable inputs from research scientists and others, governments would be able to develop a holistic perspective on the entire national R & D system—allowing policy-makers to see which areas of emerging strategic research are likely to have an impact on particular industrial sectors and whether any are likely to yield core or generic technologies.

Notes

1. In view of the size and scope of the study, it is somewhat surprising that no final report was apparently ever published. The information reported here is drawn from the first interim summary report (Sherwin and Isenson, 1966) and from a conference paper (Isenson, 1967).
2. For an excellent critical review of these studies, see Mowery and Rosenberg (1979).
3. This is often a complex process, depending not only on the internal scientific development of the research area in question, but also on developments in other fields, new instrumentation, changed industrial needs, and so on.

References

Battelle (1973), *Interactions of Science and Technology in the Innovation Process: Some Case Studies*, final report prepared for the National Science Foundation, Columbus, Ohio, Battelle Columbus Laboratories.

Bush, V. (1945), *Science, The Endless Frontier*, Washington, D.C., Public Affairs Press.

Comroe, J. H. and Dripps, R. D. (1976), 'Scientific basis for the support of biomedical science', *Science* 192, 9 April, pp. 105–11.

Gibbons, M. and Johnston, R. D. (1972), *The Interaction of Science and Technology*, final report of a study carried out for the Economic Benefits Working Group of the Council for Scientific Policy, Manchester University.

Gibbons, M. and Johnston, R. (1974), 'The role of science in technological innovation', *Research Policy* 3, pp. 220–42.

IIT Research Institute (1968), *Technology in Retrospect and Critical Events in Science*, Washington, D. C., National Science Foundation.

Isenson, R. S. (1967), 'Technological forecasting lessons from Project HINDSIGHT', paper presented at Harvard University's Technology and Management Conference, 22 May.

Langrish, J., Gibbons, M., Evans, W. G. and Jevons, F. R. (1972), *Wealth from Knowledge: A Study of Innovation in Industry*, London, Macmillan.

Mowery, D. and Rosenberg, N. (1979), 'The influence of market demand upon innovation: a critical review of some recent empirical studies', *Research Policy* 8, pp. 102–53.

Myers, S. and Marquis, D. G. (1969), *Successful Industrial Innovations*, Washington, D.C., US Government Printing Office, NSF 69-17.

Ronayne, J. (1984), *Science in Government*, London, Edward Arnold.

Sherwin, C. W. and Isenson, R. S. (1966), *First Interim Report on Project HINDSIGHT (Summary)*, Washington, D.C., Office of the Director of Defense Research and Engineering.

SPRU (1972), *Success and Failure in Industrial Innovation*, London, Centre for the Study of Industrial Innovation.

Walsh, J. (1973), 'Technological innovation: new study sponsored by NSF takes socioeconomic, managerial factors into account', *Science* 180, 25 May, pp. 846–7.

3 Research forecasting in France

3.1 Introduction

In this and the following three chapters, we analyse past attempts made in France, West Germany, the United States and Japan to undertake longer-term research forecasts and thereby to identify promising areas of strategic research. We consider their experiences as regards the accuracy and value of such exercises, and examine how the methods used have evolved in the light of those experiences. To set the scene, each chapter first looks briefly at the respective structure and organisation of state-funded science and technology in the country concerned.

In France, the situation until 1981 was that overall responsibility for science and technology lay with the Délégation Générale à la Recherche Scientifique et Technique (DGRST), which reported directly to the Prime Minister. Ministries with major research budgets included defence, industry, universities and health. The Ministry of Industry, for example, was responsible for such areas as atomic energy research (through the Commissariat à l'Energie Atomique, CEA), space research (through the Centre National d'Etudes Spatiales, CNES) and information technology. While some fundamental research was carried out by agencies such as the CEA (for example, on nuclear and solid-state physics) and INSERM, the Institut National de la Santé et de la Recherche Médicale (which came under the Ministry of Health), most was organised through the Centre National de la Recherche Scientifique (CNRS), responsibility for which lay with the Ministry for Universities.

When the Mitterrand Government came to power in 1981, a newly created Ministry of Research and Technology (MRT) took over the CNRS and certain other research responsibilities (for example, medical research was transferred from the Ministry of Health). However, in late 1982 the MRT was merged with the Ministry of Industry to form the Ministry of Research and Industry (subsequently renamed the Ministry of Industry and Research, MIR), reflecting the growing recognition of the key role played by research and development in maintaining and strengthening industrial competitiveness.[1]

In France and Germany (as we shall see in the next chapter), the organisations visited can be classified into three categories: (a) national research foundations responsible primarily for basic science; (b) ministries and other national organisations whose task is to support more strategic and applied R & D; and (c) large science-based firms. Our discussion of past and present foresight activities in France focuses mainly on the CNRS for basic science and the Ministry of Industry and Research for strategic and applied research.

3.2 Basic research: forecasting activity by the CNRS

The CNRS is a national research-funding agency responsible for all sciences, including the social sciences and humanities. Most of the research it supports is basic in nature, with only around 15 to 20 per cent of its budget allocated to applied or 'finalised' research. Besides its own laboratories, CNRS also funds a number of associated laboratories and research groups at universities. Altogether, the agency supports about 1,500 research units and employs approximately 25,000 staff. Responsibility for the different sciences is divided between seven Scientific Departments, while there are also CNRS Departments for the Use of Research in Industry, and for Scientific and Technical Information.

The CNRS operates on the basis of a rolling three-year plan somewhat similar to the Forward Look of British Research Councils. Responsibility for the preparation of this plan rests with the so-called National Committee, which is served by around forty-five discipline-based committees (some of which in turn have their own structure of subcommittees). Early drafts of the relevant sections of each year's plan are circulated to CNRS laboratories to obtain their views on new developments and priorities. The responses are then synthesised by the Director of the relevant CNRS Department, who produces a 'prospective' summarising likely research developments over the coming three to five years together with a plan for CNRS action over the next three years. These are in turn discussed and revised before being incorporated in the overall CNRS three-year plan. Thus, the main mechanism for arriving at priorities is through expert committees and discussions within the scientific community, aided in certain cases by more detailed studies of likely developments over the next three to five years in specific areas.

Because of the medium-term orientation of most CNRS plans (only in capital-intensive 'big sciences' like nuclear physics are long-term perspectives attempted), the organisation has in the past made very little use of longer-term forecasts. In the ten years up to the appointment in 1983 of Pierre Papon as CNRS Director-General, there had been only three major forecasting exercises. These focused on energy sources (the 'Hugo Report'), atomic and molecular physics (CNRS, 1980a) and solid-state physics (CNRS, 1980b). They were carried out by groups of senior scientists who in turn interacted with the relevant research communities. The report on solid-state physics, for example, was completed in 1980 by a panel of some fifteen scientists drawn mainly from CNRS laboratories and universities— industry and government agencies were not well represented, with the result that science and technology 'push' were somewhat over-emphasised at the expense of demand-side considerations. The report, which did not attempt to look more than about five years into the future, led to some reorientation of CNRS support towards surface physics and new materials, but failed to identify opto-electronics as a vital new growth area.

The report on atomic and molecular physics, also completed in 1980, was likewise concerned primarily with preparing for CNRS initiatives over the next few years, and with enabling the scientific community concerned to orientate its own research activities to broader scientific questions. While the preface to the report mentions the need to explore the likely socio-economic impact of atomic and molecular physics, either directly or indirectly through its influence on neighbouring fields (CNRS, 1980a, p. 2), the report itself devotes relatively little attention to this issue. The approach was, however, rather more systematic than that used in the solid-state physics study, with questionnaires being sent to virtually the entire research community to obtain their views on what were likely to be the important advances over the medium- to long-term future. Different topics were considered by various sub-panels, the chairmen of which then reported to the main panel. One limitation of the study was that it focused solely on French work. However, according to those whom we interviewed, it did succeed in identifying strengths and weaknesses in the country's research efforts and pinpointing possible growth areas. The report was widely read, and eventually (after lengthy discussion) had a not insignificant impact on the distribution of CNRS resources.

The largest of the three studies was the 1975 'Hugo Report' on energy sources. Despite being regarded by senior CNRS officials as the most thorough of the three forecasts, no attempt was made to use formal forecasting techniques such as scenario analysis, the report being based on expert panel discussions, along with views collected in a relatively unstructured form from the scientific community. In attempting to define a national policy for energy research over the next five to ten years, it assessed the possibilities for such new sources as solar energy, biomass and geothermal energy. Again, the emphasis was on likely technological trends, although some consideration was given to the general impacts of industrial, economic and political changes on energy demand. It concluded that research on new energy sources (in particular, solar and geothermal energy) and energy conservation should be granted priority. The report appears to have been influential in the subsequent CNRS decision to launch a new programme on solar energy research.

In the past, as these three forecasting exercises all illustrate, internal scientific and technological criteria have predominantly shaped CNRS research policy. Over time, however, it has gradually become clear, particularly in more strategic and applied areas, that external (economic and social) criteria should be given greater weight in funding decisions. This process began around 1973 with the setting up of the so-called 'CNRS clubs'. These are composed of CNRS researchers, university staff and industrialists, who meet periodically to discuss future industrial problems and attempt to identify relevant basic research that might be undertaken over the next five years or so. There are currently twenty such 'clubs', some concerned with relatively narrow areas (for example, lasers), and others with much broader fields of interest (such as oil). The 'clubs' act merely in an advisory role, making an input into the CNRS planning process. Where their advice has not been accepted in the past, this has generally been the result of opposition from academics rejecting the idea that decision-making in their field should be subject to external criteria, or claiming that members of the relevant 'club' were not fully informed on scientific matters. However, such opposition appears to be declining as the CNRS community grows more aware that future research funding may increasingly depend on demonstrating a willingness to respond to industrial and social needs.

The election of the Mitterrand Government and the subsequent appointment of Pierre Papon as Director-General of the organisation led to a further development in CNRS policy, with much greater emphasis being placed on the longer-term future. In interview with us, Papon argued that public agencies in general and the CNRS in particular have not done nearly enough long-term forecasting compared with large science-based companies. He believes that there is considerable scope for greater use of quantitative forecasting methods and of historical studies tracing recent scientific and technical trends as a means of improving CNRS's approach to identifying strategically important new areas of research. In this respect, two recent initiatives deserve mention. First, a major seminar was held in September 1983 on 'CNRS in the 1990s', at which senior CNRS staff discussed the need to adopt a longer, five-to-ten year perspective (for all areas of research, and not just in the 'big sciences' as at present).

Secondly, the CNRS has recently set up a small in-house evaluation and forecasting unit (CEP—Cellule d'Evaluation et de Prospective). One task of this unit is to develop information data bases relevant to forecasting and, in particular, to the deliberations of the 'clubs'—for example, compilations of bibliometric data on research publications and citations, patent statistics, and the results of questionnaire surveys. In addition, the unit carries out specific forecasts, for instance on the future of optics and lasers, and on growing research areas such as beta-lactamine antibiotics. In the latter, analysis of the patents for beta-lactamines listed in *Chemical Abstracts* over a recent twelve-month period revealed that no less than 45 per cent had been registered by Japanese companies. This was more than all British, French, Swiss and US firms combined (43 per cent), suggesting that Japanese industry was in the process of launching a major offensive in this sector. At the time of interviewing in 1983, CEP had only been in existence for a few months, so it was too soon to judge its overall impact. Nevertheless, confidence was expressed by CNRS officials that the background information it was starting to produce would complement and significantly improve the peer-review process used to evaluate past research and arrive at priorities for the future.

3.3 Strategic and applied research: forecasting activity by the Ministry of Industry and Research

The Ministry of Industry and Research (MIR) is currently regarded as among the most important of French ministries. It is divided into a number of divisions, including industry, energy and raw materials and research. The Research Division is responsible for approximately thirty public research organisations (*organismes*—for example, the CNRS), and for university and industrial research. The Research and Technology Directorate, in contrast, has a more 'horizontal' role, being concerned with the scientific and technological inputs to all the divisions, although it is obviously most closely related to the Research Division. Responsibility for overseeing research in different areas is divided among some fifteen departments, each handling between one and four research programmes (there are about thirty programmes in total).

The experience of the Ministry of Industry and Research with forecasting and planning in many ways parallels that of the CNRS. Until quite recently, the Ministry tended to look no more than about five years into the future. For each research programme, a rolling five-year plan (the so-called 'Schéma d'Orientation Scientifique et Technique' or SOST) is prepared, setting out current longer-term thinking on its industrial, political and social importance, and identifying priorities for research, for capital equipment, and for education. A national SOST is then produced by synthesising the thirty individual programme SOSTs. Responsibility for the preparation of the programme SOSTs rests with small groups of officials —generally researchers with an intimate knowledge of the field concerned (for example, directors of research institutes), many of whom are temporarily seconded to the Ministry for a period of three to four years. The philosophy is that, by bringing such researchers into the MIR, and confronting them with broader technological, industrial, political and social considerations (and indeed with professional forecasters—see below), they will be better able to relate research priorities to external demands on research. In addition, there is for each programme an advisory committee (about fifteen strong) made up equally from active scientists, research administrators and industrialists, the strong representation of 'users' of research ensuring that 'demand side' factors are taken fully into account in drawing up the SOST. While the SOSTs represent an attempt at systematic medium-term forecasting, Ministry officials who were interviewed admitted that they are useful more as an educative process for encouraging researchers and others to think periodically about the future than as a reliable mechanism for generating specific forecasts.

As for longer-term forecasts, there have been relatively few examples over recent years—the two most notable being on telecommunications and information technology, and on biotechnology. Both were carried out in the latter part of the 1970s at a time of increased interest in the future. However, as with the SOSTs, they were based mainly on discussions with experts rather than on the use of more formal forecasting techniques.

Towards the end of the 1970s, however, increasing inadequacies began to be recognised in the traditional mechanisms for identifying future research priorities through committees and expert discussion. In particular, the then Minister of Research, who was apparently impressed by the Japanese approach to forecasting and identifying strategic research priorities (see Chapter 6), was keen to construct a more systematic national programme for supporting innovative activity. One early result of this initiative was the 'Technology

Consultation' exercise carried out in 1979, which was very much modelled on the Japanese approach. Although still based essentially on the judgement of scientists, the approach was far more wide-ranging and thorough than anything previously attempted, with some 200 eminent researchers being asked in a questionnaire survey to predict likely future developments in their field. From their responses, which concentrated predominantly on scientific and technological trends treated independently from future social or economic needs, four major growth areas were identified:

(a) new materials;
(b) micro-electronics (particularly for robotics and communication);
(c) energy systems and conservation;
(d) biotechnology.

The results were subsequently summarised in a widely distributed booklet (70,000 copies were printed). This apparently had a significant impact, presenting as it did a broad picture of technical change and opportunities from which industry (especially smaller firms), government and the research community could all benefit. That impact was, however, more in terms of the general diffusion of information rather than of directly influencing specific policy decisions, although it did reportedly have some influence on the parliamentary debate on the 1982 research 'law' (see below).

As a result of this generally positive experience, and drawing certain lessons from the 1979 exercise, the Ministry of Research and Technology organised a second 'Technology Consultation' in 1981. This time, 1,200 experts participated, and a more systematic approach was adopted. Most importantly, a two-stage procedure was employed, the results of the first stage being used by small groups of experts to compile synthesis reports which were then circulated for comment and modification. In addition, the findings were published in a series of five detailed reports (corresponding to broad research fields—see, for example, MRT, 1982), rather than just in a summary volume.[2]

While it was felt to be too soon to judge the impact of this second 'Technology Consultation', Ministry officials stressed that it had confirmed one key lesson drawn from the first exercise—that it is relatively easy to identify the broad areas of strategic research likely to be important in the long-term future. What the MIR is finding much more difficult, however, is to translate that recognition into prompt and effective action, as this official's comments make clear:

The problem is not identifying the areas that will be important—all countries have identified the same areas [new materials, micro-electronics, energy systems, biotechnology, etc.]. The problem is to diffuse the message of the importance of these changes to industry and the civil service, and to establish the possible consequences of those changes on daily life. In particular, you have to convince the relevant firms that these are going to be the important areas, and to persuade them of the work they need to do. [Interview, 1983.]

A second and more recent initiative came at the start of 1982, when the Ministry of Research and Technology initiated a national debate on the future of research and technology and their impact on society. This had been preceded by a series of meetings and discussions among researchers extending over several years, as the scientific community had begun to mobilise against the long-term effects of static or declining budgets on their work. The combination of the election of the new Mitterrand Government committed to expansionary policies, the appointment of Chevènement as Minister of Research and Technology and a growing belief that new technologies would have immense implications for industry and society gave these discussions new impetus, and resulted in the decision to hold a 'National Colloquium on Research and Technology'. The Colloquium was organised around ten major themes, for each of which groups of eight to ten experts were commissioned to produce discussion papers. In addition, over thirty regional colloquia were held beforehand to discuss more regionally focused reports. Papers were prepared at the end of these discussions, and delegates chosen to attend the National Colloquium. Industrialists, trade unionists and politicians were among those who contributed, along with researchers. The results of the discussions at the Colloquium were then synthesised, yielding seven priorities:

(a) the production and rational use of energy and other sources of energy;
(b) biotechnology;
(c) mastery and development of electronics;
(d) the technological development of French industry;
(e) scientific research and technological innovation in the service of lesser developed countries;
(f) research into employment and improvements in working conditions;
(g) promotion of the French language in science and the wider dissemination of science and technology as part of French culture.

Whereas the first three priorities were essentially discipline-based, the others were more concerned with broader techno-economic and 'political' questions. The fourth and seventh priorities, for example, apparently reflected Chevènement's own personal interests, while the sixth stemmed from the close involvement of trades unions in the 'Great Debate'. A few months later, in July 1982, these priorities were enshrined in a law laying down 'Guidelines and a Programme for Research and Technological Development in France'. (Besides establishing these seven priorities, the law made provision for an annual examination and evaluation of research by parliament, as well as for the representation of public interests in various organisations concerned with research and technology. It also established action programmes relating to basic research, certain 'finalised' research areas and various well established technologies like nuclear power and space technology—see Kellermann, 1984, p. 219, for further details.)

Although a great deal of effort was certainly expended in this wide-ranging and democratic approach to identifying priorities, the process of arriving at the final list was, in the view of some of those interviewed, not as systematic as it might have been.[3] This is borne out by the fact that robotics and new materials were not originally included, although their importance has since been recognised by funding increases matching those for objectives (a), (b) and (c) above.

While the Technology Consultations and the National Colloquium represented more formalised attempts to identify promising areas of research than anything seen previously, they both depended ultimately on the traditional mechanism for arriving at research priorities, namely the judgement of scientists. By 1982, however, it had become clear that new methods of research forecasting were required, particularly in arriving at strategic decisions on the distribution of resources between different fields. In that year, Chevènement decided that, in the light of the new Government's policies towards industry and the increased responsibilities of the state that they implied, a 'think tank' should be established to provide advice on longer-term strategic issues. A new Centre de Prospective et d'Evaluation (CPE) was therefore established.

Among the functions of the CPE are (i) the evaluation of research activities in France; (ii) monitoring research developments worldwide (for example, a network of observers is being built up in Japan and elsewhere); (iii) commissioning (or in some cases carrying out) scientific and technological forecasts; and (iv) ensuring that the results of (i) to (iii) are diffused through government and industry (for example, through seminars). The CPE does not come under any of the MIR divisions, but reports directly to the Minister and his staff. It does, however, provide inputs to MIR departments and programmes. The aim is to enable the officials responsible for the operation of programmes (and for the drawing up of the SOSTs) to become better informed about the methods, problems, scientific prospects and economic and social implications of the research concerned. Professor R. Chabbal, Head of the Research and Technology Directorate at the MIR, was a particularly strong advocate of this scheme, arguing in an interview with us that the opportunities which it creates for bringing professional forecasters into contact with senior decision-makers, and with researchers temporarily seconded to the MIR to help run research programmes, have enabled the Ministry to improve significantly its foresight activities and decision-making.

At the time of interviewing, the CPE had only been in existence for a year and had yet to decide upon a formal methodology for approaching its task. As a result, it was still exploring various approaches—drawing on the advice of experts and committees, experimenting with Delphi techniques, and commissioning forecasts in specific areas from universities and consultancies.[4] For example, between 1982 and 1983, a study was carried out by the Observatoire Français des Techniques Avancées (OFTA) on 'The Economic Impact of New Technologies in the Year 2000'.[5] This was based largely on interviews conducted with relevant experts. Although the officials whom we interviewed were unable to point to any direct impact of the study, it was seen as having had an indirect influence in terms of enabling government officials and others to understand, in some cases for the first time, the nature and implications of the new technologies, and hence to appreciate their strategic importance.

Also created in 1982 (as part of the French response to the international Versailles Summit) was the Centre d'Etudes des Systèmes et des Technologies Avancées (CESTA). One section of CESTA incorporated the Institut de Prospective des Sciences et de Prévision Technologique (IPSPT), which was charged with responsibility for providing scientific and technological forecasts to the MIR. Unlike the Centre de Prospective et d'Evaluation, CESTA is an independent public body, although it reports to the Ministry through the CPE.[6] Under the IPSPT, twelve programmes were set up to examine the effects of technological change on society (see CESTA, 1982, for details), including one ('Techno 2000') which has the specific task of providing technological forecasts in certain priority sectors (for example, telecommunications, biotechnology, etc.).

Like the CPE, CESTA has experimented with various approaches to forecasting (for instance, with scenario analysis), but it has tended to rely principally on discussions with researchers, industrialists and policy-makers. And as with the CPE, it was unfortunately still too soon at the time of interviewing to judge the likely impact of CESTA forecasts. Of the MIR officials interviewed, some expressed optimism about the CPE and CESTA, but others were more qualified in their enthusiasm, arguing that strategic decisions relating to the distribution of resources should be based not on formal forecasts but on a continuing dialogue between researchers and the users of research (especially in industry). One official expressed his reservations as follows:

The key thing is to have here in the Ministry senior researchers—both basic scientists and applied scientists—who are still active in research—this is the best method for selecting priorities. They have the best ideas as to which are the most promising fields. You have to 'plug' them into the system rather than relying on professional forecasters. By having good scientists here in the Ministry for up to four years (they then *have* to leave), we can expose them to decision-makers, and also to forecasters (for example, in the CPE)—this is perhaps the most productive approach to identifying promising new areas of research . . . Forecasting must *not* be done by isolated groups of forecasters working alone. But if you bring together researchers, decision-makers, and forecasters right from the start, then the forecasts are likely to be useful. [Interview, 1983.]

3.4 Forecasting activity by industry

Although only one French company could be visited in the course of the study reported here, its experiences in relation to long-term forecasting are nevertheless not without interest. Company A was selected because of its involvement in a wide range of high-technology sectors, including advanced electronics, telecommunications and medical equipment. In line with its emphasis on advanced technology products, the company devotes approximately 15 per cent of its revenue to R & D. Of this, 95 per cent is spent on R & D carried out in the company's divisions and subsidiaries, while the Central Research Laboratory, which is principally engaged in more basic research, accounts for the remaining 5 per cent. The company's overall R & D activities are coordinated by a Committee for Technical Management.

The main mechanism for determining longer-term priorities (for the next five to twenty years) is the annual 'Orientation Plan', which, although non-quantitative, gives researchers in the Central Research Laboratory an indication of the areas felt to be important to the company's future, and provides management with an idea of likely technological developments. To prepare the plan, the Central Research Directorate first solicits scientists in the various research laboratories for their views on preferred lines of future research—the scientists have to prepare submissions and make oral presentations in support of their proposals. At the same time, management in the different divisions are interviewed about the longer-term problems that they face. (It has been found that the divisions tend first to focus on relatively short-term difficulties, and have to be prompted to explore the underlying longer-term problems.) There is then an exchange of information between the two sides, with meetings being held at which senior scientific personnel (the top thirty or so group leaders in the Central Research Laboratory) try to relate the proposed 'menu' of projects to the company's long-term needs—in other words, attempting to mesh together scientific and technological opportunities with market demands that the company has the capacity and skills to meet. On the basis of these discussions, the 'Orientation Plan' is then drawn up.

Until recently, Company A operated a very small in-house forecasting unit (consisting of one permanent member of staff, aided by occasional PhD students), the main role of which was to collect and synthesise background information to aid corporate decision-making. The unit undertook a limited amount of generally qualitative forecasting although it also commissioned more quantitative studies from outside consultancies (especially on future market trends). While the unit did provide regular inputs into the annual 'Orientation Plan', the company still tended to rely mainly on the views of senior management and researchers in determining the areas of research likely to be of future importance. Thus, when its director recently retired, the unit was disbanded after some twenty years of existence.

In discussing the reasons why the unit had not been continued, it was stressed by the research directors that most of the company's R & D resources are allocated to applied research and product development, where short- and medium-term market criteria tend to predominate in decision-making. Longer-term forecasting is of relevance only in helping to set priorities for basic research, which, as noted earlier, accounts for only about 5 per cent of the company's R & D budget. In identifying new lines of longer-term research, the policy since the disbandment of the forecasting unit has been to set aside some 10 per cent of the strategic research budget at the start of each year. This is then used to investigate promising ideas put forward by researchers during the course of the year. Provided the proposed research falls in the general area of the company's interests, and provided the cost is less than 200,000 francs (about $25,000), the researcher is encouraged to carry out a 'quick and dirty' experiment to test the feasibility of the idea. It is accepted that perhaps 80 per cent of these experiments will fail, but the remaining 20 per cent are seen as providing the source of some of the company's most innovative developments.

Overall, Company A seemed relatively satisfied with the existing procedure for determining research priorities, and examples were given where it had succeeded in the early identification of important new research areas (for instance, the company was one of the first to spot the potential of integrated optics). At the same time, it was admitted that the procedure is by no means perfect. It takes up considerable time on the part of central management and scientists, and the recommendations are not always implemented. One notable example concerned nuclear magnetic resonance (NMR) technology. NMR scanners were identified relatively early as a potential growth area in the 'Orientation Plan', but the medical equipment division, unconvinced by the predictions, failed to act upon them, despite pressure from central management. It was only after the Central Research Laboratory had itself initiated work in the area (apparently against the wishes of the medical equipment division) that the division became convinced of the potential of NMR technology. Hence, in this case, the 'Orientation Plan' succeeded in identifying this important new research area, but the company failed to act as quickly as it might have done.

In short, Company A remains sceptical about the utility of more formal approaches to long-term forecasting. The former forecasting unit was seen as having had a beneficial psychological effect in terms of keeping everyone 'on their toes', and of ensuring that staff from different parts of the company were brought together periodically and forced to discuss a particular theme. The disbanding of the unit and the unwillingness to experiment with more formal forecasting techniques was justified on the grounds that the tradition of centralised decision-making in France makes the likelihood of major shifts in industrial policy with each change of government very great, thereby largely invalidating many of the demand-side assumptions on which have been based the long-term predictions as to the research areas likely to prove of strategic importance to the company. Despite such recent initiatives as the National Colloquium, an unfavourable contrast was nevertheless drawn between the 'top-down' approach to R & D forecasting and planning still seen as predominant in France, and the 'bottom-up' approach with strong industrial participation favoured in Japan. This is clear from the following statement:

In France, there has been a tradition of centralisation since the seventeenth century, which has meant that bureaucrats make the choices. They may seek advice from researchers and industry, but only to further their preconceived ideas. Some of them may be trained scientifically, but they do not have experience in applying research to market-orientated problems. Later in their careers, some may move to industry, but virtually none go from industry to government. So they have no experience of industry and industry's needs. The general result is that decisions are no better than 50 per cent good. The other 50 per cent you could get equally well by throwing dice! . . . This is very different from the approach of the Japanese. They rely very heavily on industry to do prospective studies and to push particular research interests. [Interview, 1983.]

To sum up, we have seen in this chapter how, prior to the start of the 1980s, ministries and other state agencies in France appear to have made relatively infrequent use of long-term forecasts for identifying strategically important areas of basic research. However, since the election of the Mitterrand Government, there has been increased enthusiasm for foresight activities in science, with the adoption of more systematic and broadly based approaches (as in the National Colloquium) and the establishment of various forecasting units in the CNRS and MIR. In contrast, the enthusiasm of industry seems, if the experiences of Company A are typical, to have waned over the same period precisely because the state has been adopting a more 'interventionist' role than in previous years. As we shall see in the following chapter, experience in West Germany represents in some respects a mirror image of that in France as the Federal Republic has moved from a Social Democrat to a Christian Democrat administration.

Notes

1. For further details of the organisation of French science and technology, and of recent changes in its structure, see, for example, the useful review article by Kellerman (1984). Shortly after the drafting of our book was completed, the Ministry of Industry and Research was redivided into two. However, most of the discussion in section 3.3 still applies to the new Ministry of Research and Technology.
2. At the time of interviewing in 1983, the summary report for the 1981 Technology Consultation was still being prepared.
3. Indeed, none of those interviewed was able to explain exactly how the first three priority areas were selected—it seems to have been more a matter of informal collective intuition than anything very rigorous.
4. The CPE also works closely with CESTA (see subsequent text) and with other organisations concerned with the longer-term future (for instance, planners in the Commissariat Général du Plan).

5. OFTA has also recently completed a study for the Commissariat Général du Plan entitled 'Les Enjeux Technologies des Années 1985–90', but at the time of writing this had yet to make any formal impact on decision-making.

6. In fact, the missions of the CPE and IPSPT are very similar, several of those interviewed in 1983 being uncertain as to what was intended to be the relationship between the two, since no clear division of labour seemed to have been established.

References

CESTA (1982), Centre d'Etudes des Systèmes et des Technologies Avancées, Paris, CESTA.

CNRS (1980a), *Rapport de Prospective: Physique Atomique et Moleculaire*, report of CNRS working group, Paris, Délégation Générale à la Recherche Scientifique et Technique.

CNRS (1980b), *Rapport de Prospective: Physique de la Matière Condensée*, report of CNRS working group, Paris, Délégation Générale à la Recherche Scientifique et Technique.

Kellerman, E. W. (1984), 'France: a logical attitude to science', pp. 212–26 in M. Goldsmith (ed.), *UK Science Policy*, Harlow, Longman.

MRT (1982), *Le Sol et ses Resources*, Thème 4, Consultation Technologie, Paris, Ministère de la Recherche et de la Technologie.

OFTA (1983), *Les Enjeux Technologiques des Années 1985–1990*, étude réalisée par l'Observatoire Français des Techniques Avancées pour le Commissariat Général du Plan dans le Cadre des Travaux Préparatoires au 9e Plan, Paris, Commissariat Général du Plan.

4 Research forecasting in West Germany

4.1 Introduction

The mechanisms for government support of research are more complicated in West Germany than in France, with several ministries funding and carrying out scientific and technological activities. Of these, by far the most important is the Federal Ministry of Research and Technology, followed by the Ministries of Defence, Economics, and Education and Science. Support for academic basic research is largely channelled through the Deutsche Forschungs-gemeinschaft (DFG) which acts primarily as a research foundation. It is complemented by the Max-Planck-Gesellschaft which operates institutes in areas of basic research where a more focused approach is necessary than is possible in dispersed university departments. In addition, a network of thirteen National Research Centres[1] is responsible for most of the country's 'big science' facilities, the centres receiving some 90 per cent of their funds from the Federal Ministry of Research and Technology (BMFT). BMFT is also responsible for the support of more industrially related R & D, as is the Fraunhofer-Gesellschaft (FhG) through its various applied research institutes. The organisations visited in West Germany can be classified in essentially the same way as in Chapter 3, and each will be considered in turn.

4.2 Basic research: forecasting activity by the DFG and MPG

4.2.1 *Deutsche Forschungsgemeinschaft (DFG)*

The DFG is an autonomous organisation whose members include universities, research institutions, the various academies of science and other scientific associations. Its primary task is to provide financial support across the entire range of basic research from the humanities to engineering (its other tasks include encouraging co-operation between researchers, providing advice to the Federal and state governments (Länder), and fostering closer relations between West German scientists and their international colleagues), and for this it receives grants-in-aid from the Federal Ministry of

Education and Science and the Länder (totalling around DM900 million in 1983).

The DFG employs a number of mechanisms for supporting research, the main one being the so-called 'normal procedure' which accounts for some 40 per cent of its overall budget. Under this, scientists apply for support for specific research projects (or for fellowships, travel costs, etc.). The DFG does not attempt to carry out forecasts in relation to such work (details of the research support for 'normal procedure' grants are not even included in the DFG 'Grey Plans' described below—see DFG, n.d., p. 31). One rather unusual feature of the 'normal procedure', however, is that the peers used by the DFG to judge proposals are elected by the research community, with secret ballots being held every four years.

A second important mechanism consists of 'priority programmes', in which scientists from several institutions work on joint co-ordinated research for approximately five to ten years. Priority programmes were introduced in the early 1950s to help restore West German science to international standards in selected fields and to train a new cadre of research scientists. Although in theory such programmes constitute a more direct form of support than the 'normal procedure', in practice the initiative for new lines of research still rests largely with the scientific community, with proposal pressure being used to alert DFG officials to emerging research opportunities. In deciding whether to set up a particular priority programme, the DFG convenes an expert group to report on the state of the field concerned and the international standing of West Germany within it. The group surveys developments over the past five years, and attempts to look forward over a similar period in order to identify the likely scientific prospects. The emphasis is very much on internal scientific requirements and opportunities rather than the relationship of the proposed research to broader technological, economic and social goals. A draft plan is then submitted to the DFG Senate and subsequently revised in the light of its comments. Finally, the DFG notifies all interested researchers of the new initiative and invites the submission of applications for funding.

Whereas priority programmes involve collaboration between researchers working in several different locations, the third procedure employed by the DFG—'special collaborative programmes' —provides support for collaborative research within a single university or between neighbouring universities and research institutes. Such programmes tend to be set up in areas requiring a multi-disciplinary research effort lasting up to fifteen years. Again, however, the initiative for setting up such programmes effectively arises outside DFG—in this case, generally from individual universities—and the peer-review process used to decide among competing programme proposals concentrates primarily on their respective scientific merits.

Besides these three main mechanisms, the DFG offers two other forms of research support: (i) core funding for 'research groups' (multidisciplinary groups of researchers typically collaborating for a period of six years); and (ii) the operation of central research facilities (for example, oceanographic research vessels). Proposals for a new research group or central facility are dealt with in a similar manner to those for priority programmes.

Because the various research-support mechanisms have traditionally depended to a greater or lesser extent on relatively uncoordinated initiatives from outside DFG, there is clearly a danger that potentially important research areas may be neglected. In an effort to devise a more systematic approach to policy-making, the DFG in the late 1950s prepared the first of its 'Grey Plans' (published in 1961). To date, there have been seven such plans, each focusing on a medium-term horizon of three to four years. The earliest were constructed by DFG officials on the basis of written suggestions from elected referees, the draft plan subsequently being discussed and revised by the DFG Senate. For the fourth and fifth Grey Plans, a more elaborate procedure was employed in which committees were set up to analyse the future for various fields. However, a feeling that government was taking insufficient interest in these detailed plans, and in particular the arguments they put forward to support requests for appropriate funding, has led the organisation to revert to a simpler procedure whereby early drafts are prepared by DFG officials after consultation with elected referees and others, and after taking into account the reports of the expert groups set up to consider new programme applications.

The DFG officials interviewed by us reported that, while there have been other attempts by the organisation to improve its methods for longer-term forecasting and planning, these have also tended to be concerned with more effective identification from a purely scientific view of potentially interesting research areas. One example was a report published in the early 1970s (DFG, 1971) which recommended improved procedures for the planning of new research—for instance, through the use of questionnaire surveys. However, when these were first employed by DFG, it was discovered that researchers tended to couch their replies in terms of individual research interests rather than what were really felt to be growth points in science. As a result, the next time questionnaires were used, groups of experts had to be convened to interpret (or 'clean up') the findings. This, however, proved rather cumbersome, and it was decided in future to dispense with questionnaires and rely solely upon the traditional procedure of expert discussion.

Overall, then, the criteria used by DFG to identify promising new lines of research have up to now been almost wholly related to internal scientific considerations. This approach has been possible because the level of resources available has been such that there has been little competition between fields. The DFG essentially reacts to proposal pressure mediated by the quality-control function provided by the peer-review system, although the role of DFG officials can also be important since they are well placed to discern trends both from their day-to-day contacts with scientists and from proposals submitted under the 'normal procedure'. While the DFG (like the scientific community) strongly favours this flexible approach, and has thus far eschewed any attempt to base funding on forecasts incorporating long-term industrial and economic needs, it recognises the approach's limitations. One such limitation occurs in the case of newly emerging research areas (often involving cross-disciplinary interaction) where no peers exist to whom the DFG can turn for advice. (An example of this occurred a few years ago with the new field of synergetics, where the German pioneer in this area had to turn to other sources of funds because DFG initially failed to appreciate its importance.)

Another and more fundamental limitation with the existing approach is the difficulty in deciding in any systematic way *which* fields should be given preferential support. This problem, the resolution of which may entail bringing external factors directly into consideration in decision-making, has yet to be fully confronted. It is, however, recognised that the present system of deciding on proposals by judging their individual scientific merits will no longer be feasible or acceptable to the scientific community once the demand for resources begins to exceed substantially the funds available, as seems destined to happen in the near future. Instead, some more systematic procedure for arriving at inter-field priorities will almost certainly have to be instituted, and for this formal forecasting techniques may well be required.

4.2.2 *The Max-Planck-Gesellschaft (MPG)*

The Max-Planck-Gesellschaft supports some fifty research institutes, and in 1983 had an overall budget of just under MD1 billion mainly provided through grants from the Federal and Länder governments. It finances basic research, attempting to bridge the 'gaps' left by

DFG support for academic research—for example, in areas where research is technically complex and requires expensive capital equipment and large specialised scientific teams. MPG activities are organised within three sections: (i) physics, chemistry, and technology; (ii) biology and medicine; and (iii) the social sciences and humanities. Overall responsibility for co-ordination of research priorities is vested in the MPG Scientific Council, with more specific research-planning responsibilities handled by the Planning Sub-Committee of the MPG Senate. In effect, however, the Sub-Committee's task can be seen largely in terms of responding to initiatives from the scientific community. (Further details can be found in MPG, 1977.)

Each year, the MPG receives about twenty proposals for new institutes. While some can be rejected immediately by MPG officials, the rest are subject to critical review by respected scientists in the research community. The MPG may also consult the DFG in cases where the latter already has an interest in the field concerned. At the end of this informal vetting procedure, an average of one or two applications typically remain which merit more detailed consideration. The Senate Planning Sub-Committee is then asked informally if the proposal(s) should be forwarded to the relevant MPG section(s) for further consideration. The Sub-Committee is so constituted that it should have the expertise to make such a decision, the inclusion of overseas members ensuring that advice from foreign experts can be readily obtained. Once a proposal has been formally put before an MPG section, a commission is set up to decide whether it should be rejected or recommended to the MPG Senate. The MPG generally looks first to its own scientists to make up the commission, but where there are insufficient in-house researchers, experts from universities and industry may be recruited. In addition, efforts are normally made to bring in foreign experts, particularly from the United States and Britain. In general, commissions concern themselves solely with the intrinsic scientific merits of proposals rather than their longer-term technological or economic significance.

In all the discussions surrounding a proposed new institute, the MPG President plays a key role. By sitting in on the commission set up to consider a particular proposal, the President is able to gauge the strength of the arguments for and against a new initiative. Indeed, it is the task of the commission to make a convincing case that the new institute is essential. Similarly, when a commission is established to decide whether an existing institute should be closed (for example, when the 'founding-father' director is about to retire), the President plays an active role, asking the awkward questions that other memebers of the commission might otherwise prefer to ignore. Indeed, the President may first set up a preliminary presidential committee to provide background briefing on the important questions to put before the commission. In short, the philosophy of the MPG over the years has been to give overall responsibility for policy-making to its Presidents, while ensuring that they are able to call upon the best possible advice.

A central feature of the MPG is the relative operational autonomy granted to its institutes and to their directors. As a result, one of the main criteria in determining whether a new institute should be established (or an existing one should continue after the retirement of its current head) is whether a suitable director can be found. Where the scientific case for a new institute is strong but there are doubts about the ability of the proposed director, the MPG has over the last ten years made use of an alternative procedure whereby a much smaller research group is first set up. The leader of the group is then given a period of five years in which to demonstrate whether he or she would make an effective director of a permanent institute. Since this mechanism was initiated, four such research groups have been supported, three of which were subsequently upgraded into institutes (for example, the Institute of Quantum Optics), while one was closed at the end of the trial period.

Although initiatives for setting up new Max Planck institutes generally originate from within the research community, there are exceptions. One concerns the establishment of the Institute for Polymer Research. During the 1970s, the DFG began to realise that the prevailing pattern of support for polymer research based on dispersed groups at different universities might be a key reason why Germany had lost its former dominant position in the field. The DFG concluded that a large interdisciplinary institute should be created—larger than could be financed and serviced by a single university. The German Science Council then became involved. (The Council, which is made up of researchers and scientific administrators as well as some industrialists, politicians and others, coordinates research policy between the Länder and the Federal Government.) A panel of experts was appointed to consider the future of polymer research over a period of up to twenty years. The panel in turn sought the advice of other experts, concentrating primarily on likely scientific advances in polymer research, and taking somewhat for granted that long-term economic benefits would arise. Its report concluded that Germany should increase the level of support for polymer research, and that this would best be accomplished through the establishment of a large interdisciplinary institute. Since it was felt that the new funds should be concentrated on basic research, the panel recommended that the proposed institute should come under the aegis of the MPG rather than the Fraunhofer-Gesellschaft. After preliminary discussions within MPG, the proposal was placed before the section for physics, chemistry and technology, which subsequently recommended in favour of establishing an Institute of Polymer Research.

In this particular example, there was at least some consideration of economic factors in deciding whether to set up the new institute; industry was extensively consulted, the three main chemical companies in Germany all apparently believing that basic polymer research should for strategic reasons be carried out within the MPG system, since this would provide them with a supply of well trained scientists as well as access to results of the research on new materials. In most cases, however, the MPG, in judging applications for new institutes, is concerned predominantly with the scientific merits of the research area and whether scientists of the highest calibre are available to head and staff the proposed institute. Nevertheless, there are signs that the MPG is beginning to pay more attention to the question of science and technology-transfer to industry. For example, some interest was expressed during our interview with senior officials in the results of a study recently commissioned by BMFT from the Swiss consultancy firm, Prognos A.G., on how the Japanese arrive at policies for integrating basic research with more applied R & D. However, considerable scepticism was still voiced about formalising any further the policy-making process within the MPG on the grounds that any benefits from attempting to forecast the long-term technological and economic benefits from particular research areas are likely to be more than outweighed by the loss of flexibility associated with the present, relatively informal system.

4.3 Strategic and applied research: forecasting activity by the BMFT and FhG

4.3.1 Federal Ministry for Research and Technology (BMFT)

Any discussion of foresight activities by BMFT must be seen in the context of the Ministry's multi-faceted role in the West German R & D system. With a budget of around DM7 billion in 1983, BMFT is responsible for (a) organising and funding research in 'high technology' sectors such as nuclear energy and aerospace; (b) supporting industrial R & D through a variety of mechanisms including direct and indirect subsidies to firms, and financing special initiatives (such as in information technology); and (c) maintaining a scientific infrastructure (for example, supporting a central biotechnology laboratory and several big science centres, as well as providing core funds to the MPG and FhG and paying the subscriptions for various international research organisations).

Although a certain amount of specialised long-term planning activity is carried out within BMFT divisions and by the central planning group, the organisation operates predominantly on the basis of a rolling four-year plan. In preparing its budget for the coming year, the BMFT is constrained by the fact that some 80–90 per cent of its resources will already be tied up in the form of long-term projects and permanent commitments. For the remainder, bids are submitted by the various BMFT divisions. Since their total cost invariably exceeds the funds available, a 'bargaining' process then takes place to reduce the proposed commitments to the ceiling figure previously set for the overall BMFT budget by the government. To a certain extent, the task of prioritisation starts at the bottom with the identification of the lowest priorities—the research that is not felt to be of international quality, or which has no apparent relevance to industrial needs. To assist in this task, a check-list of criteria is used: for example, is the research ripe for private industry to take over? Is it an area of applied research where the scientists have become diverted into more basic research? (If so, it may be suggested that they apply to the DFG for future funding.) Up till now, by weeding out low-priority proposals in this way, the BMFT has generally found that it has sufficient resources to fund the remaining promising research topics.

As for longer-term forecasting of strategic research, the following BMFT official's comments were not untypical:

In my view, we undertake *no* long-term forecasting of strategic research. What we do have is a very spontaneous and unstructured process—a self-balancing process based on political infighting and bargaining . . . It is partly because the BMFT began as an Atomic Energy Ministry, and we have still not developed proper mechanisms to function as a Research and Technology Ministry. [Interview, 1983.]

This is not to imply, however, that no long-term planning is carried out within BMFT. In areas of high technology characterised by lengthy periods of capital-investment, the BMFT has to look to the longer-term future—around ten years for aerospace projects, and up to twenty years or more for atomic energy programmes.[2] Similarly, in the case of 'big sciences' like high-energy physics, the fact that the time-scale in building and exploiting new research facilities may be ten to twenty years has again called for an element of longer-term planning. For example, in 1981 an expert committee (the Pinkau Commission) was charged with establishing priorities for a range of possible new facilities in nuclear and particle physics and in various other fields such as geology and oceanography. According to BMFT officials interviewed by us, the Commission was concerned primarily with the likely scientific impact of the facilities.[3] It made little use of formal forecasting techniques, instead arriving at consensus on priorities more through a somewhat pragmatic process of mediating between the interests of the relevant research communities.

Aside from high technology and big science, most longer-term forecasting by BMFT is relatively restricted in scope. There has, for example, been no equivalent as yet of the Pinkau Commission for strategic and applied research—i.e. no wide-ranging attempt has been made to address such questions as: what are the strategically important research fields? And which fields should West Germany fund? Instead, forecasts have tended to be carried out in specific areas already identified as important (through informal discussions etc.), the main purpose of such exercises being to help BMFT develop appropriate research programmes. For example, in a study of materials science carried out at the start of the 1970s, various experts were asked to look ten to fifteen years into the future in order to identify emerging new fields of research. The study yielded suggestions as to how to sponsor and organise research, the results being incorporated in a programme of materials science set up shortly afterwards. The exercise was repeated some five years later, and again in 1983. In each case, the emphasis has been on identifying underlying technological trends, but some attempt has also been made to take account of economic and industrial considerations.

Other examples of long-term BMFT forecasts have tended to be even narrower in focus—for instance, a study of the prospects for ultrasound in the field of medical technology over the next ten years. This was carried out for BMFT by Prognos A.G. at the start of the 1980s. The Prognos team consulted experts around the world on the current state of research in the field, on likely improvements in the hardware and in associated diagnostic techniques, and on potential markets. They were thus able to identify certain 'gaps' in knowledge and hence a number of research priorities (for example, the imaging of smaller human organs), which were subsequently incorporated within a new BMFT research programme.

In the field of information technology, BMFT has commissioned several studies from consultancies such as Arthur D. Little, SRI International and International Data Corporation. These have generally yielded five-year perspectives, with only a very hazy picture for the period between five and ten years into the future (because of the extremely rapid pace of technical change in the areas concerned). One example was a study of multi-computer systems by SRI in 1981. Among the questions addressed were the following: what is the future for multi-computer systems, and which of the various options are likely to be adopted? What is the present 'state-of-the-art'? Where are the most important research groups, and what are their plans for the coming years? As in the ultrasound study, the work was carried out by a small group of consultants (each already knowledgeable in the field) who held extensive discussions with experts in several countries. Economic and industrial factors were taken into account along with scientific and technological considerations, and again the results were used by the BMFT in establishing a promotional programme.

A second and somewhat different example in the field of information technology is represented by a study of data-processing carried out jointly by SRI International and Arthur D. Little International. The main element in this study was an evaluation of three BMFT programmes on data-processing (covering the period 1967–79), the results of which then formed the basis for various recommendations concerning BMFT support over the next five years. The approach adopted in the evaluation involved analysing the original goals of the BMFT programmes, comparing them with the results achieved, evaluating the various mechanisms used for implementing the programmes and assessing the overall impact of the Ministry's activities in the area (c.f. Matthes, n.d., p. 6).

The information examined came not only from relevant reports, statistics and the technical literature, but also from researchers and experts in industry. In analysing future prospects, the study group drew up a list of key factors—for example, the probability of attaining particular goals, the costs and benefits of the methods used, West Germany's position in relation to other countries, and the extent of existing initiatives by private companies which, suitably weighted, enabled them to identify the key growth areas and main opportunities for the West German computing industry. As in other forecasts, the results were utilised by BMFT in preparing a new programme of research support in the field.

Besides these relatively narrow forecasts within particular research fields, BMFT has on one occasion attempted to carry out a much broader survey to identify 'white spots' (or growth points) across the spectrum of research and technology. An applied systems group (the Arbeitsgruppe für Angewandte Systemanalyse, ASA) was set up to look from ten to twenty years into the future using the whole gamut of systems analysis techniques.[4] In the opinion of BMFT officials, however, the group failed completely in its search for 'white spots'. It ended up doing traditional technology assessment, and was disbanded in 1982 (AGF, 1983, p. 6). The lesson drawn from this episode is that forecasting should not be carried out by professional forecasters in isolation from scientists in the areas concerned.

Another reason why BMFT has not done more in the way of longer-term research forecasting is perhaps a belief within the organisation that its heavy reliance on peer-review committees, together with other frequent contacts between its programme officers and the scientific community, enables it to remain sufficiently abreast of research developments. However, probably a more important reason is related to the intrinsic structure of the West German R & D system. Although BMFT underwrites a significant proportion of the MPG's budget, and supports several of its own basic research centres (the thirteen National Research Centres, for example, each receive 90 per cent of their funds from BMFT, the remainder coming from the Länder), basic research nevertheless enjoys a very high degree of autonomy. There has thus been no incentive for BMFT to under-take wide-ranging forecasts of promising scientific areas because there is little possibility of getting them adopted by a basic science community concerned with protecting the freedom from outside interference accorded to them under the post-war West German Constitution. In the opinion of several of those interviewed, there is, therefore, a fundamental structural problem in integrating priorities for basic research (parts of which have clear strategic potential) with those for more applied R & D. This has been re-cognised by the present Minister for Research and Technology who, in a recent lecture, pointed out the need to 'set new priorities in areas of application-oriented research where there is a particularly large growth of knowledge in the corresponding basic research sector, for example, biotechnology' (Riesenhuber, 1982).

On the other hand, the election of the Christian Democrat Govern-ment has at the same time led to pressure on BMFT to pursue a less 'interventionist' role,[5] at least in relation to industrial research. For many years, there has been continuing debate between the Social Democrats and the Christian Democrats about the extent to which the state should intervene in industrially related research. The Social Democrats contend that public funds should be used to *direct* industrial R & D, and that research support should be em-ployed as a vehicle for intervening in investment decisions and in strategically influencing the nation's industrial structure. The

Christian Democrats deny that this is an appropriate role for the state, believing instead that entrepreneurs should be left to decide on their own criteria whether to develop particular new lines of R & D—if no market exists for the resulting technology, the state should not intervene to create one artificially. A central disagreement thus exists over the relative emphasis BMFT should give to direct research intervention (through financing individual industrial R & D projects etc.) compared with indirect support (via subsidies to firms hiring new scientific and technical staff, tax-relief for research expenses etc.), with the Christian Democrats much preferring the latter. Over recent years, BMFT has therefore had to reorientate its technology policy and budgetary structure to reflect the views of the new government, in particular devoting more of its resources to providing support (both financial and infrastructural) to initiatives originating within industry (cf. BMFT, 1983). As one official put it: 'it is not the aim of this department at present to *identify* the important new technologies, but to provide mechanisms whereby the state can support initiatives taken by industry— i.e. *companies* decide what are the important areas' (interview, 1983).

The BMFT has therefore had to adjust to the fact that the current government is not overly enthusiastic about long-term planning, being sceptical about its value and predictive reliability. The approach at present is to leave strategic decisions on R & D as far as possible to industry and the market.

4.3.2 *Fraunhofer-Gesellschaft (FhG)*

The FhG operates a network of thirty research institutes, the main task of which is to carry out applied research for government and industry. On average, just over 30 per cent of institute budgets (which totalled DM310 million in 1983) is made up of core funds from the Federal government, while the remainder is earned through contract research (approximately half for the Federal government and Länder and half for industry). Core funds are used for preparatory research in areas where support is felt likely to be forthcoming from government contracts in one-to-two years' time and subsequently from industry. Under the FhG system, institute directors are accorded considerable autonomy, and are responsible for ensuring that their staff retain over the long term the capacity to move flexibly into new areas of potentially marketable R & D as and when they emerge. Central funding from FhG, together with certain types of government contract (for example from BMFT), is thus used as 'risk capital' to create this research capability.

As noted above, FhG institutes on average earn 70 per cent of their income from contract R & D. In general, the FhG only sets up a new institute if it is confident that this 70 per cent figure will be reached within five years. One recent example was the decision to establish the Institute for Solar Energy. In the late 1970s, a group working in a defence-research institute found themselves unable to follow up certain aspects of their work that were felt to have commercial potential. They approached the FhG President, who initiated a process of consultation with industry, the BMFT and others about the possibility of a new solar energy institute. Examination of work at universities and existing institutes revealed a comparative lack of research activity in the area. As a result, an advisory committee was set up by the FhG to explore the matter in more detail. The committee attempted to look up to five years into the future, and, although it concentrated on likely technical trends, economic and industrial factors (such as potential markets) were also considered. Eventually, after thorough consultation with the relevant experts and detailed discussions within the organisation, the FhG Senate decided to set up a research group initially. This was given a year in which to prove itself and was subsequently expanded into an institute.

Thus, the mechanism involved in arriving at the decision to create the Institute for Solar Energy was extensive discussions with the scientific community and industry, with the FhG endeavouring to involve the leading experts in the field. (And, as with the establishment of MPG institutes, the role of the President was apparently central.) The same approach was adopted in a more recent study as to whether the FhG should set up a new group to carry out micro-electronics research on very-large-scale integration (VLSI). The study was carried out by two experts, who reported to an advisory committee. After consultations with researchers, industry, BMFT officials and others, and discussions within the FhG Senate, it was decided to create a research group in 1982. In this case, the Federal government agreed to provide funds for five years until the group was able to earn 60–70 per cent of its income from contract R & D.

Because of the requirement that its institutes obtain two-thirds of their income from contracts, forecasting by the FhG tends to adopt a medium-term perspective and to focus on more applied research; i.e. what research will meet *existing* needs, or those over the next one to five years, rather than long-term needs? Furthermore, since decisions as to which areas should receive core funds are left largely to institute directors, the role of the FhG is more that of co-ordinating activities between institutes (to avoid unnecessary duplication, for example) rather than picking future scientific winners. Indeed, no long-term forecasts of promising areas of science were reported by those interviewed as having been undertaken. This said, the FhG has in the past commissioned various studies from the Institute for Systems Technology and Innovation Research (ISI) at Karlsruhe. However, these have tended to be small and very specific in focus. For example, in 1979 ISI spent two months studying the possibilities of using electro-chemical devices for energy-storage. Based on interviews with virtually all the West German experts in the area, the study, which focused on the next five to ten years, considered both economic and technical factors. Although the study did generate some background information and the Institute for Solar Energy is now carrying out research on this topic, in general the FhG does not regard the ISI studies as having been particularly successful in terms of their impact on policy or research. FhG officials admit that this may have been partly because ISI did not have a sufficiently clear idea about how the FhG planned to use the findings, but perhaps a more fundamental problem is that the researchers in the fields concerned felt no sense of commitment to the ISI results. Consequently, rather than commissioning forecasting studies from outside groups, the FhG now prefers to carry out its own forecasts aided by committees of experts.

Finally, it is worth mentioning that the FhG has in the past attempted bibliometric analysis of the research literature to identify the most productive scientists. However, this has sometimes been found to yield misleading results and is not regarded as particularly useful. The following comment perhaps best sums up the current views of the FhG in relation to the possibility of improved forecasting techniques:

There may be some scope for increased use of systematic interviews and other formalised forecasting techniques, but this has to be done in parallel with discussions with researchers. It may provide background information, but you cannot make decisions solely on that basis. There has to be a political commitment to implement the results and you can only get that by fully involving the scientists. They get this in Japan by involving everyone in the discussions and generating a sense of political purpose. [Interview, 1983.]

4.4 Forecasting activity by industry

Although the three West German firms interviewed operated in markedly different industrial sectors (the automotive, electrical and electronics, and chemical sectors), they have in common a very systematic and thorough approach towards long-term planning. All the information available in the scientific literature, the technical and industrial press, and patent and other data banks (for example, the Lockheed data base) is routinely examined in order to monitor scientific and technological trends and thereby help frame corporate R & D strategy. Nevertheless, there are some important differences between their forecasting activities, arising from the divergent nature of their business activities.

Company B is a large automotive manufacturer with an R & D budget equivalent to some 3–4 per cent of turnover. In large part, this is devoted to development; only 8 per cent of the R & D budget is devoted to research, of which 80 per cent is spent on comparatively applied work relating to vehicles and engines with only 20 per cent being devoted to more basic research in physics, chemistry and materials science. The fact that, at least until fairly recently, the pace of technological change has been relatively slow in the automotive industry is probably the main reason why comparatively little is spent on longer-term strategic science. The identification of new lines of research is left mainly to scientists within the research department. The procedure is that proposals are discussed with engineers in the development departments that will eventually become responsible for the work, and for its incorporation in new products and production processes. In some cases, the scientists concerned are then encouraged to take the idea further. If the subsequent results are promising, further resources will be made available, but, if they are not, recommendations will be made that other lines of research be pursued. In addition, the overall research budget is the subject of annual discussions between representatives of the research department, the various development departments and a member of the company's Board.

Until a few years ago, longer-term planning was largely decentralised within the company's different divisions, a situation which sometimes gave rise to disputes that had to be resolved at board level. However, in 1980, a central planning group was set up to co-ordinate planning between the divisions, and this now consists of some fifty staff. Although most corporate planning is concerned with the next five to eight years, longer-term perspectives of up to twenty years (corresponding to the life-cycle of vehicles from the earliest design work to final sales) are also attempted. However, because this newly formed group is necessarily still in the process of building links with planning groups in the various divisions, its long-term forecasts have as yet had relatively little impact on corporate research strategy.

Over the last fifteen years, planners within Company B have experimented with a variety of approaches to long-term forecasting. Econometric techniques were tried and rejected, as was portfolio analysis. In the 1970s, the company even attempted to apply the world model developed by Forrester at MIT to predict automotive markets, again without success. In the light of these experiences, the company has concluded that quantitative techniques for long-term forecasting are generally unsatisfactory, and it has instead concentrated on qualitative approaches, especially scenario analysis. Scenarios were first employed in the mid-1970s, and since then there has been an appreciable learning process as the approach has become more sophisticated and the data employed more accurate. (The planners now look back with some amusement at their early scenarios!) One conclusion that has been reached in relation to scenario analysis is that the company cannot meet all its forecasting requirements in-house, and it currently employs a wide range of consultants. When considering very general questions, the company often utilises multi-client studies purchased from consultancies and for slightly more focused questions studies may be specially commissioned, leaving only the most specific questions to be tackled completely in-house. Scenario analysis now constitutes an integral element of Company B's longer-term strategic planning, although it is used more in relation to predicting future demand patterns than promising scientific developments.

Company C has a wide variety of product-lines ranging from large electrical installations to advanced micro-electronics. It spends just over 9 per cent of sales on R & D, with 86 per cent of the R & D budget being devoted to product and systems development, 9 per cent to production engineering methods, and 5–6 per cent to 'application-oriented research'. Longer-term research, together with development work that is best carried out centrally, is performed in the corporate research and technology divisions, the budget of which constitutes approximately 13 per cent of the company's total R & D expenditure. The remaining 87 per cent is spent on R & D within the operating groups. The largest item of corporate R & D expenditure is on micro-electronics, which accounts for about 40 per cent of the total.

Decisions on corporate R & D are arrived at by relating proposals submitted by researchers to the company's long-term strategic plans, the latter being based on a combination of estimates of future markets, an assessment of the company's abilities and an appraisal of its competitors' probable plans. The proposals put forward by researchers are first discussed at various levels within corporate

R & D to yield a preliminary list of priorities. Discussions are then held between corporate R & D and the operating groups in order to arrive at priorities and an overall research strategy. The principal mechanism involved is a multi-stage iterative process based on a series of discussions, with final responsibility for producing a research programme and budget resting with the R & D Committee of the Managing Board. This committee consists of the heads of the operating groups, together with those of the corporate divisions of research and technology, finance, and sales and marketing. It is chaired by the company's Chief Executive Officer.

According to the staff interviewed (in the Technology Division), Company C tends not to use formal scientific and technological forecasts in arriving at decisions on longer-term strategic research— it relies on general discussions of new products and processes and of overall trends, but without normally resorting to formalised scenario-analysis except on the demand side (for evaluating market trends, for instance). Within the Technology Division, there is no long-term forecasting group. The possibility of establishing a forecasting group has been raised in the past, but discussions with firms that do have such groups have led Company C to doubt whether the resulting forecasts are worth the effort involved. The company, however, does place great emphasis on monitoring scientific and technological trends and the R & D activities of competitors through the operation of a large patenting office of 300 staff. With the aid of a computer, staff are very quickly able to examine the scientific patent literature and thereby make an analysis of particular research areas.

One reason given by Company C for not using forecasts to identify promising areas of scientific research is that the time-horizon associated with the implementation of a new technology is strongly sector-dependent. It was argued that for micro-electronic components, perhaps the most heavily science-based area, the technology is advancing so rapidly that it is often impossible to look more than about five years into the future, whereas large power-generation plants may take ten years to plan and operate for thirty to fifty years. It was therefore doubted whether a formalised approach to identifying strategically important new areas of research could cope with the divergent technological demands of the company's different operating groups. Instead, forecasts of the company's future technological needs tend to focus around individual products and product groups. Recently, a new and more formalised procedure for establishing those needs was introduced.

For each of the company's products, a list is first drawn up of the main technologies involved—there are generally between ten and twenty for a given product. Next, a chart is plotted showing the relative importance of each technology against the company's position for that technology in relation to its competitors.

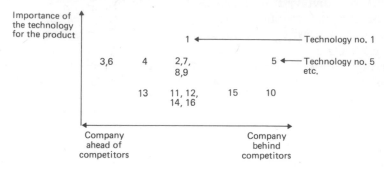

Figure 4.1 Technological needs versus technological strengths: R & D priority-setting by Company C

The information required to construct these diagrams is generated through questionnaires administered to the company's researchers and marketing staff. The analysis is carried out for hundreds of the firm's products, and the results fed into a computer, which is then used to identify the company's technological strengths and weaknesses. At the time of interview, this procedure had been operating for only a short period, so it was difficult to judge its success (particularly since the first questionnaire used by the company had to be substantially revised). However, those interviewed were optimistic that this systematic approach could yield potentially valuable information on the basic technologies in which the company needs to strengthen its R & D efforts.

The forecasting experiences of Company D, one of West Germany's leading chemical firms, are particularly instructive, perhaps because of the rapid change over recent years in the knowledge-base of the industry. In the latter part of the 1970s, the company set up a strategic planning group to provide a central service to the operating divisions. In carrying out project briefs, the group, which currently consists of a nucleus of about fifteen staff, is normally aided by staff from relevant divisions (including researchers, managers and salesmen—there are generally about fifty or sixty at any one time, thereby ensuring that strategic planning is well integrated with other corporate functions) and sometimes by outside consultants. Certain members of the strategic planning group are responsible for research forecasting. The general approach adopted is to monitor all relevant scientific and technological information[6] (especially in technical and industrial journals), and hence to identify where new ideas and trends are emerging. If it is suspected that these new developments are likely to be important to the company, they are then subject to more detailed analyses and forecasts. This may involve paying for computerised on-line literature and patent searches (for example, to establish exactly what research has already been carried out, or to predict which companies are likely to be the main competitors). Alternatively, in-depth studies may be commissioned from consultancies such as SRI International or Nomura when a more complete overview of a particular field is required.

As with Company B, experiences with research forecasting have involved a gradual learning process. Initially, it took rather long to produce each forecast, but the process has steadily been speeded up at the same time as being made more thorough. The company stressed how difficult the learning process had been in arriving at a satisfactory level and balance in its scientific forecasting efforts. It had become apparent, for instance, that it is impossible to forecast globally (i.e. across the entire spectrum of research) and continuously. This is because of the vast effort—in obtaining the necessary information, carrying out interviews and discussing the results with interested parties—required to generate accurate predictions that can stand up to rigorous cross-examination by the company's Board. To be of most use, forecasts need to be highly specific, and they must only be undertaken after they have been requested by the relevant operating division, as the following statement makes clear:

Forecasting should only be carried out when a need for it is expressed starting at the bottom— for example, when our Division of Plastics is analysing its future opportunities. Then you can carry out a forecast of something *specific*. General forecasting without the pressure and demand from the existing business is not accepted in an organisation like ours. It is a case of the prophet being out of time. No one listens to his prophecies. Only if a part of the organisation is carrying out a hard analysis of the future will information from technological forecasts be really valued, discussed and used. If a forecast stands alone as a prophecy, no one will care for it. [Interview, 1983.]

In other words, the company first selects those areas of new technology that appear to hold out greatest promise for corporate growth, and then tries to predict how they will evolve over coming years, analysing and following discrete development lines. The results of such forecasts were reported as having proved increasingly useful, and have gradually become accepted as a vital part of the company's planning process not only for R & D but also for its strategic planning in general. Most importantly, research staff now appreciate the value of forecasting, and are willing to participate fully, providing the feedback to improve the accuracy of the forecasts and the commitment to ensure that ultimately the forecasts are successfully fulfilled—something which they were not always willing to do when technological forecasting was first introduced and had yet to become an integral part of corporate strategic planning.

This chapter has described how in West Germany, as in France, relatively few attempts have been made to identify areas of research with long-term strategic importance. In the case of the organisations responsible for the support of more fundamental research (i.e. the DFG and MPG), this reflects the strongly cherished belief that initiatives should be left to the scientific community. In the case of strategic and applied research, the low level of foresight activities reflects a number of factors. One is that both BMFT and FhG are primarily concerned with the medium-term rather than the longer-term future. Secondly, in BMFT's case, it may be partly attributable to the failure of the 'white spots' search. Lastly, the election of a Christian Democrat government has over recent years resulted in some decentralisation to industry of the responsibility for initiating new lines of strategic research, thereby reducing the need for forecasts by BMFT. On the other hand, we found evidence of extensive foresight activities in the companies visited. Moreover, the level of such activities has apparently increased significantly during the 1980s as firms have come to appreciate the benefits that a systematic approach to research monitoring and forecasting can yield, especially in relation to longer-term corporate planning. In Chapter 5, we shall see that certain similarities exist between West Germany and the United States, in particular the belief that responsibility for identifying promising areas of basic science should be devolved largely to the research community, and the adoption of a relatively sophisticated approach to foresight activities in certain companies.

Notes

1. During the study, we also visited the Association of National Research Centres (AGF), which co-ordinates the R & D activities of the thirteen laboratories and promotes the interchange of information and experience. Although the AGF is not directly involved in research forecasting, the Director was able to give useful background information on foresight activities undertaken elsewhere in West Germany.

2. One example of a long-term forecast is provided by the Häfele Report on fast-breeder reactors undertaken in the early 1970s. At the time, the national research centre at Karlsruhe was looking for future projects, and the development of fast-breeder reactors was seen as a suitable undertaking for the laboratory. The forecasts contained in the Häfele report have subsequently proved somewhat inaccurate.
3. The same holds true for a similar study carried out by a group headed by H. Maier-Leibnitz in 1975.
4. It was originally intended that the size of this group should grow to over thirty. However, because of various institutional and personnel difficulties, the number employed never exceeded twelve.
5. Besides the effect of the change in government described here, there has also been a public reaction to the country's fast-breeder programme, which is widely seen as absorbing too high a proportion of government R & D resources. The failure of industry to contribute towards the costs of the programme on the scale originally anticipated has led BMFT to become much more wary about entering into major research commitments in the absence of firm support from industry at a very early stage.
6. In particular, information-gathering networks are operated in the United States and Japan, and anything relevant is translated and sent back to West Germany.

References

AGF (1983), *Arbeiten zur Systemanalyse und Technologiefolgenabschätzung in der AGF*, Bonn, Arbeitsgemeinschaft der Grossforschungseinrichtungen.

BMFT (1983), *BMFT Budget for 1983*, summary and translation prepared by the British Embassy, Bonn, available from the Overseas Technology Information Unit (document no. 83/3023), UK Department of Trade and Industry.

DFG (1971), *Forschungsplanung*, Kolloquium über Forschungsplanung, Wiesbaden, Franz Steiner Verlag.

DFG (n.d.), *Deutsche Forschungsgemeinschaft: Organisation and Functions*, Bonn, DFG.

Matthes, K. (n.d.), 'Experience gained with methods for the evaluation of R & D programmes in the Federal Republic of Germany, mimeo, Bonn, BMFT.

MPG (1977), *The Max-Planck-Gesellschaft and Its Institutes: Portrait of a Research Organization*, Munich, Max-Planck-Gesellschaft.

Riesenhuber, H. (1982), 'New accents in research policy', lecture given to Fraunhofer Society, October 21, mimeo, Bonn, BMFT.

5 Research forecasting in the United States

5.1 Introduction

A wide variety of mechanisms for the support of research exists in the United States, reflecting a post-war pattern of scientific growth in which several federal agencies have developed significant research programmes. For our purposes, the US R & D system can be characterised in terms of (i) the National Science Foundation (NSF) which has traditionally funded most areas of curiosity-orientated research, and which, together with bodies such as the National Academy of Sciences (NAS), is responsible for the direction of a large part of US basic academic science; (ii) other federal agencies such as the Departments of Energy (DoE) and Defense (DoD) which support some fundamental science but are concerned primarily with research of a strategic and mission-orientated nature;[1] (iii) federal bodies charged with overall management and control of government-funded R & D, most importantly the Office of Science and Technology Policy (OSTP) and the Office of Management and Budget (OMB); (iv) science-based industrial firms; and (v) technical consultancy firms. Let us consider each of these in turn.

5.2 Forecasting in basic science: NSF and NAS

The National Science Foundation (NSF) was set up in 1950 as an independent agency of the Federal Government. It is charged with promoting and advancing scientific progress (in all areas of science apart from clinical research) in the United States. This it does primarily through sponsoring scientific research and supporting initiatives in science and engineering education. (For a detailed discussion of the mandate and operational activities of NSF, see Ronayne, 1984, pp. 115–24. Since Ronayne also gives a useful summary of the overall structure of science and technology in the United States, and of the roles of OSTP and NAS, the details are not repeated here.)

The National Science Board (NSB), which is made up of a Director and twenty-four members (all of whom are appointed by the President), is the policy-making body of the NSF. In addition, the Board

is responsible for approving all major new programmes. Most proposals for support are, however, dealt with at a lower level within
the agency. The Foundation is organised into various directorates,
each headed by an Assistant Director. The directorates are in turn
divided into between four and six divisions (an organisational chart
can be found in NSF, 1981, p. 76). The distribution of resources
among the directorates is determined not so much on the basis of
any formal priority-setting techniques as through a process of negotia-
tion between the Assistant Directors (cf. Ronayne, 1984, p. 117).
The latter rely primarily on inputs from the scientific community
either directly through expert committees (or from the periodic
field surveys discussed below), or indirectly in the form of 'proposal
pressure', which is regarded as a particularly useful indicator of
shifting research priorities.

Although the set of criteria formally used by the NSF in determining which projects to support include 'utility or relevance' and
'effect of the research on the infrastructure of science and engineering' (NSF, 1981, p. vii), the NSF officials interviewed felt that
intrinsic scientific criteria should be foremost. They argued against
the imposition of explicit external criteria (such as long-term economic value) to prioritise different areas of research on three main
grounds: (i) while fundamental science does indeed have a major
impact on technology and the economy, this is long-term and cannot
be predicted;[2] (ii) it is the role of mission-orientated agencies to
identify and fund more strategic and applied research, and the role
of industry to support work with identifiable economic returns;
and (iii) no research of major long-term importance goes unfunded
because, even if NSF turns down a particular proposal, another
agency is very likely to provide support.

5.2.1 *The COSPUP field surveys*

As we shall see in section 5.4, the question of whether the NSF
should make greater attempts to identify priorities among its
activities[3] is currently under discussion because it is clear that certain
areas of basic science are providing increasingly crucial inputs to
emerging technologies. The last occasion when science was subject
to such re-appraisal was during the first half of the 1960s. At that
time, there

was a crisis in relations between Congress that came to a head in 1963. Among
the many causes of this unhappy state of affairs . . . [was] increasing awareness
that the exponential growth of federal research and development expenditures
could not continue at the same rate and that there was a consequent need for

developing better priorities for the allocation of science resources . . . [Kofmehl, 1966, p. 112.]

In an effort to head off the mounting criticism of US science policy, the House Committee on Science and Astronautics appointed a Subcommittee on Science, Research and Development in August 1963. This was given 'responsibility for overall evaluation of research and development throughout the United States, . . . [and] for achieving the most effective utilization of scientific and engineering resources to accomplish national goals' (ibid., p. 113).

At the same time, the National Academy of Sciences[4] decided that it needed to improve its working relations with Congress, and in December 1963 an agreement was concluded with the Committee on Science and Astronautics under which NAS would provide advice to Congress on science-policy issues (cf. ibid., p. 114). As its first task, NAS was asked to carry out a study, one of the two tasks of which was to consider: 'what level of Federal support is needed to maintain for the United States a position of leadership through basic research in the advancement of science and technology and their economic, cultural, and military applications?' (quoted in ibid., p. 114).

NAS assigned responsibility for the study to the Committee on Science and Public Policy (COSPUP). COSPUP had been established (under a different name) in 1962 following discussions in which the NAS President (Dr D. Bronk), Dr G. B. Kistiakowsky (former Special Assistant for Science and Technology to the US President) and Dr J. B. Wiesner (Kistiakowsky's successor) had figured prominently. As NAS members, all three wished to see the Academy playing a more central role in policy-making at the highest levels, in particular within the Executive (cf. ibid., p. 107).

To carry out the study requested by Congress, COSPUP set up a 'Panel on Basic Research and National Goals'. Of the Panel's fifteen members, only two were drawn from industry, the remainder being academic researchers. Not surprisingly, therefore, the Panel's report, entitled *Basic Research and National Needs* (COSPUP, 1965), was more persuasive in discussing scientific needs and identifying scientific opportunities than it was in considering their economic applications and how to achieve 'the most effective utilization of scientific and engineering resources to accomplish national goals'. Nevertheless, the report was extremely influential in terms of shaping overall US policy towards the support of basic science over the next fifteen years, just as a parallel report two years later on *Applied Science and Technological Progress* (COSPUP, 1967) helped establish a framework for government support of applied science.

While both these reports clearly had a major impact, it was apparent from the start that they needed to be complemented by more specific studies. In particular, COSPUP's Chairman, Dr G. B. Kistiakowsky, in the light of his experience as a former Presidential Science Adviser, felt that the availability of periodic surveys of individual research fields would do much to improve science policy-making (cf. Lowrance, 1977, p. 1254). He was therefore instrumental in initiating a series of field studies which were funded by the NSF and various other agencies with basic research responsibilities, and which were mainly published between 1964 and 1974. The areas covered included astronomy (Whitford, 1964; Greenstein, 1972), chemistry (Westheimer, 1965), life sciences (Handler, 1970), materials science (Cohen, 1974), physics (Pake, 1966; Bromley, 1972) and plant sciences (Thimann, 1966). (Summaries of the surveys can be found in Lowrance (1977), together with an analysis of their impact and shortcomings.) Since this series of surveys represents what is still one of the most interesting attempts to look at the longer-term future for science, we shall consider them in some detail. In particular, we highlight how one of the original aims of examining the wider economic and social impact of different scientific areas in order to help determine overall national research priorities was obscured (if not totally lost).[5] Instead, the scientific community seized upon the surveys as a new means of bringing to the attention of the public the 'outstanding opportunities' confronting their fields and hence arguing for increased support.

The field surveys nevertheless served a number of useful purposes. First, they provided an opportunity for scientists to think systematically about the state of their field, and the relationship of their own particular research area to the field as a whole. (The comprehensive reviews that resulted were of particular benefit in the more diffuse or less centralised fields like materials science and plant sciences.) Secondly, many of the scientists involved were for the first time forced to confront policy issues—how to wrestle with priorities, how to interact with government officials—so the surveys had an educational effect. Thirdly, as noted above, they provided a platform from which to educate government, industry and the wider academic community as to the potential benefits from these fields, and to mount a case for appropriate levels of funding.

On the negative side, however, the reports in general (and we discuss two notable exceptions later) suffered from certain major shortcomings. First, because they were mostly produced by committees of eminent scientists (aided by panels of other senior experts), they tended to reflect existing institutional or 'elite' interests. Associated with this was a second problem: the surveys came to be seen by some (particularly those in government) as little more than public-relations exercises for individual fields—inevitably concluding that there was a need for significantly increased funds— rather than serious attempts at facing up to the future.[6]

Thirdly, the surveys tended to adopt an over-academic approach, some taking unduly long to complete and yielding massive tomes (for example, the Bromley Report took thirty months and Volume I alone ran to more than 1,000 pages). According to government officials interviewed, this was one reason why the reports had much less impact than they might. Related to this was a fourth problem —the fact that the committee and sub-panel approach used was inevitably rather expensive: the Bromley Report reportedly cost approximately $2 million (not counting the significant investment of senior scientists' time).

Fifthly, the approach used was best suited to established, coherent and well organised 'big science' fields like astronomy and physics. It was far less satisfactory for diffuse 'little sciences', and in particular for newly developing areas straddling several disciplines (for example, fields like robotics). This gave rise to certain criticism: as Lowrance (1977, p. 1257) notes, 'those who resent the self-serving nature of the surveys always mutter something like, "to those who have, more will be given".'

The sixth shortcoming was that most of the surveys, and particularly the earlier ones, concentrated principally on questions of intrinsic scientific merit rather than the relationship of different research areas to techno-economic and social questions, even though, as we have seen, there was considerable public concern with such questions at the time the COSPUP surveys were launched. The Westheimer (1965) Report, for example, blithely asserted that chemistry research was useful without attempting to identify *which* areas of chemical research were more likely to be useful than others.[7] The comparative neglect of the technological and industrial implications was perhaps inevitable given that this survey committee, like many others, consisted almost entirely of university academics—a failing now recognised by senior US officials as the source of many of the structural weaknesses associated with this genre of surveys of the future for science.

The lack of industrial involvement is partly responsible for the final and arguably most important problem with the COSPUP surveys—their general failure to identify future priorities within the fields studied.[8] The usual assumption was that research budgets would continue to grow as rapidly as previously (typically around

20 per cent per annum) and that funds would be forthcoming for new research areas identified as important through the peer-review system. The implications of reduced growth rates were largely ignored.[9] Of the various reasons for this, one was a desire to avoid offending colleagues by judging some research areas less worthy of support than others; a second stemmed from the constitution of committees—with 'delegates' representing the main specialty areas—which made such a task extremely difficult; and a third was the fear of generating self-fulfilling prophecies about decreased growth rates. Lowrance, in his useful analysis of the COSPUP field surveys, has these comments to make about the strategy of avoiding discussion of alternative budgetary possibilities:

While this freigning may have had some marginal advantages, there is no evidence that it influenced the construction of the federal budget. Indeed, it simply denied potentially useful guidance to the science-sympathetic officials who, in any event, had to wage the budgetary infighting, with or without advice. [Lowrance, 1977, p. 1259.]

Despite these criticisms and the implication that responsibility for identifying strategically promising areas of science cannot be left entirely to the scientific community, a learning process was undoubtedly involved, with two of the later COSPUP studies yielding interesting lessons about research forecasting. The first was the Bromley Report (1972). Stung by the accusation that physicists were incapable of identifying priorities, the Bromley Committee undertook an experimental jury-ranking exercise to determine the emphasis that committee members felt should be given to different research areas over the next five years in terms of (a) the internal intellectual needs of physics, and (b) the likely impact of physics on other sciences, applied research and technology. Extensive discussions were first held within the committee to agree upon appropriate criteria. These were followed by consultations with sub-panels to divide the eight main physics specialties into sixty-nine programme areas. Committee members then confidentially ranked each programme area in terms of the agreed criteria on a ten-point scale.

Figure 5.1 shows the criteria used (for example, 'potential contribution to technology' (no.8) or 'potential for immediate applications' (no.9)) and the results for the main physics specialties. Figure 5.2 presents more disaggregated data on programme areas within optics, while Figure 5.3 compares the sixty-nine programme elements in terms of intrinsic and extrinsic merits. Clearly, the programme areas in the top right corner of the latter table—for example, lasers and masers (programme element 1)—which were ranked highly in

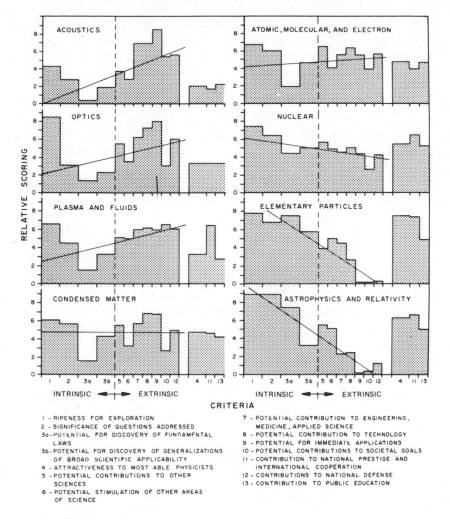

RELATIVE SCORING

INTRINSIC ◄─┼─► EXTRINSIC   INTRINSIC ◄─┼─► EXTRINSIC

CRITERIA

1 - RIPENESS FOR EXPLORATION
2 - SIGNIFICANCE OF QUESTIONS ADDRESSED
3a - POTENTIAL FOR DISCOVERY OF FUNDAMENTAL LAWS
3b - POTENTIAL FOR DISCOVERY OF GENERALIZATIONS OF BROAD SCIENTIFIC APPLICABILITY
4 - ATTRACTIVENESS TO MOST ABLE PHYSICISTS
5 - POTENTIAL CONTRIBUTIONS TO OTHER SCIENCES
6 - POTENTIAL STIMULATION OF OTHER AREAS OF SCIENCE

7 - POTENTIAL CONTRIBUTION TO ENGINEERING, MEDICINE, APPLIED SCIENCE
8 - POTENTIAL CONTRIBUTION TO TECHNOLOGY
9 - POTENTIAL FOR IMMEDIATE APPLICATIONS
10 - POTENTIAL CONTRIBUTIONS TO SOCIETAL GOALS
11 - CONTRIBUTION TO NATIONAL PRESTIGE AND INTERNATIONAL COOPERATION
12 - CONTRIBUTIONS TO NATIONAL DEFENSE
13 - CONTRIBUTION TO PUBLIC EDUCATION

Source: Bromley (1972, p. 404).
Note: The straight lines superposed on the histograms are drawn simply to provide a characteristic signature for each subfield. It is interesting to note that these signatures divide naturally into three classes, with emphasis shifting from intrinsic to extrinsic areas as the subfield matures.

Figure 5.1 Bromley Survey Committee ratings of core physics subfields in terms of specified intrinsic and extrinsic criteria

terms of both intrinsic and extrinsic criteria, would seem to have represented priority areas for funding. However, when it came to interpreting the judgements for policy purposes, the Bromley Report claimed rather feebly that the exercise was not one of 'prioritisation' but of 'programme emphasis'; since judgements as to 'programme emphasis' were likely to change rapidly, it was argued that it was

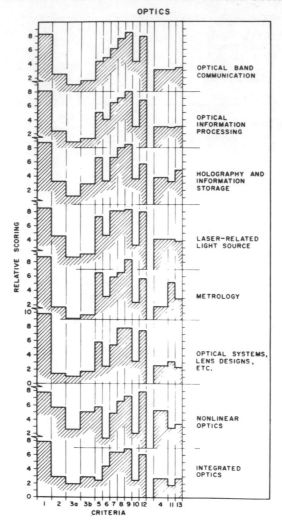

Source: Bromley (1972, p. 406).
Note: The criteria 1–13 are listed under Figure 5.1.

Figure 5.2   Bromley Survey Committee ratings of programme elements within the optics subfield in terms of specified intrinsic and extrinsic criteria

therefore inappropriate to draw any firm conclusions other than the fact that physicists *could* prioritise.

While the Bromley findings are without doubt interesting, they would almost certainly have been more successful if they had been combined with those of a panel of researchers drawn from science-based firms, thus enabling the 'science-push' perspectives of academic

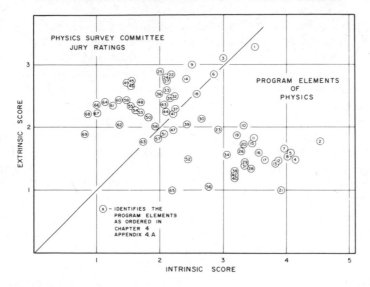

Source: Bromley (1972, p. 414).
Note: The key for the numbered circles can be found in Appendix 5A in Bromley (1972, pp. 445–6). To take some of the more interesting examples: (i) programme elements 1 and 3 (ranked highly in terms of both intrinsic and extrinsic criteria) correspond to lasers and massers, and quantum optics respectively; (ii) 2, 4, 5, 7, and 8 (high intrinsic but relatively low extrinsic merit) relate to programme elements in the field of particle physics; (iii) 64, 66, 67, and 68 (low intrinsic but relatively high extrinsic merit) relate to programme elements in the field of acoustics; (iv) 65 (relatively low intrinsic and extrinsic merit) corresponds to slow neutron physics.

Figure 5.3 An extrinsic versus intrinsic map summarising Bromley Survey Committee ratings for sixty-nine programme elements in eight core physics subfields

physicists to be linked with the 'technology-pull' perspectives of industrial researchers. This is well illustrated by the example of integrated optics (programme element 58), which was ranked fairly low in terms of both intrinsic and extrinsic criteria, when in fact it has subsequently developed into a strategically important scientific area.

The other COSPUP review containing results of methodological interest is that on materials science and engineering (the Cohen Report, 1974). In many respects, this review represents a model of how to survey the prospects for an individual field. Not only was there a good balance in the committee between industry (twelve members) and academics (ten),[10] but the report took seriously the task of establishing priorities, and there were none of the usual glib demands for major increases in funds.

The study began by examining the future challenges facing those industrial sectors dependent upon materials science, analysing the expected areas of technological development. The committee then attempted by means of a postal questionnaire to identify the areas of basic and applied research likely to play an important role in those future technological developments. A total of 555 usable responses were received from experts in industry (who accounted for about 40 per cent of replies), academia and government. The questionnaire listed some fifty specialties in materials science and engineering, classified into three categories: (a) properties of materials; (b) classes of materials; and (c) processes for materials. Respondents rated each specialty on a scale from 0 to 100 according to the priority they felt it deserved for basic research and for applied research. Some of the results are shown in Table 5.1 and Figure 5.4.

While the findings are not without relevance even after ten years (for example, the high priority accorded to ceramics and composites anticipated the subsequent rapid growth in these areas), and demonstrate what can be achieved by bringing together researchers from industry and academia, their impact on US research policy was reportedly not as great as might have been expected. This may be because of the reputation earned by previous COSPUP surveys, or because materials science was regarded at the time as a low priority within basic research. Nevertheless, the study deserves scrutiny in any contemporary attempt at identifying promising areas of science.

Before moving on to consider various studies commissioned by the NSF from outside consultancies, it should be noted that, in the most recent round of field surveys (the Brinkman Report on Physics, the Dickinson Report on Geological Sciences, the Pimentel Report on Chemistry and the Schmitt Report on Engineering, all of which had yet to be published at the time of writing), many of the above criticisms have been taken into account. One senior government official commented as follows:

We politely pointed out the shortcomings of previous studies in early meetings with the Steering Committee [for one of the above reports] and some of these have been rectified. . . . I think that it is now well recognised that science-based industry people should have a major role in such studies. [Private correspondence, 1984.]

It is, however, far too soon to judge how successful these latest field reports will prove.

5.2.2 *NSF studies commissioned from consultancies*

During the mid-1970s, influenced perhaps by the somewhat unsatisfactory experiences with the COSPUP field surveys, the NSF decided, as part of a comprehensive effort to develop a long-range planning process, to experiment with different approaches to

Table 5.1 Cohen Survey Committee priority ratings for basic research in materials science and engineering

Specialty	Familiarity of respondents (%)	Priority for basic research (%)
Properties of materials		
Atomic structure	61	68
Microstructure (electron microscope level)	54	69
Microstructure (optical microscope level)	61	53
Thermodynamic	60	64
Thermal	54	57
Mechanical and acoustic	60	70
Optical	48	61
Electrical	55	66
Magnetic	45	52
Dielectric	43	52
Nuclear	41	60
Chemical and electrochemical	49	70
Biological	20	56
Classes of materials		
Ceramics	54	72
Glasses and amorphous materials	52	68
Elemental and compound semiconductors	47	62
Inorganic, nonmetallic elements and compounds	50	59
Ferrous metals and alloys	58	59
Nonferrous structural metals and alloys	53	63
Nonferrous conducting metals and alloys	51	57
Plastics	40	65
Fibres and textiles	28	46
Rubbers	24	42
Composites	45	70
Organic and organo-metallic compounds	28	51
Thin films	43	62
Adhesives, coatings, finishes, seals	33	58
Lubricants, oils, solvents, cleansers	23	43
Prosthetic and medical materials	21	54
Plain and reinforced concrete	21	31
Asphaltic and bituminous materials	16	27
Wood and paper	20	30
Processes for materials		
Extraction, purification, refining	43	60
Synthesis and polymerization	33	61

Table 5.1 (*cont.*)

Specialty	Familiarity of respondents (%)	Priority for basic research (%)
Solidification and crystal growth	59	66
Metal deformation and processing	49	56
Plastics extrusion and moulding	29	43
Heat treatment	58	55
Material removal	44	51
Joining	47	61
Powder processing	43	56
Vapour and electrodeposition, epitaxy	43	58
Radiation treatment	35	55
Plating and coating	42	55
Chemical	39	51
Testing and nondestructive testing	62	71

Source: Cohen (1974, p. 193).

identifying research areas of long-term promise. An internal 'task force' was set up in 1977 to consider these questions, subsequently commissioning three studies from Arthur D. Little, Battelle and Technical Audit Associates with the overall objective of 'improving techniques for understanding the relationships between basic research and technological needs in a prospective fashion'. An internal NSF memorandum at the time noted that

the use to NSF of these possible techniques will be to provide additional background information on the potential benefits to the nation of important advances in basic research. By attempting to connect (1) the industrial perceptions of technological needs with (2) the scientific perceptions of research opportunities that may affect technological capability, we may detail more clearly the relevance of basic research to technological opportunities. [NSF internal memorandum, 1977.]

In the first of the studies, Arthur D. Little was asked to focus on industrial perceptions of technological opportunities and relevant basic research (Arthur D. Little, 1977). Six sectors including both high and low technology-based industries were selected for detailed examination (pharmaceuticals, semiconductors, automotive products, wood-based fibres, instruments and communications). The approach adopted was a novel one, with 'relevance trees' being constructed to 'illustrate the linkages between selected objectives . . . [in these] industry sectors, and the technological options, research approaches

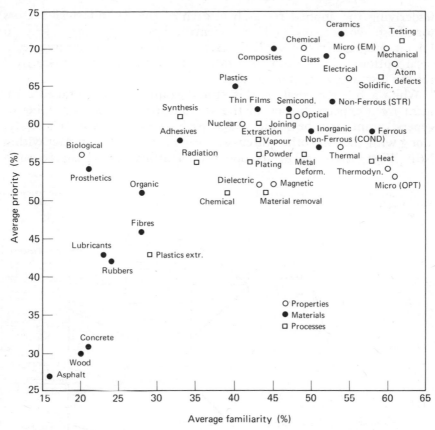

Source: Cohen (1974, p. 197).

Figure 5.4 Basic research in various materials specialties: Cohen Survey Committee priority ratings versus familiarity ratings of respondents

and basic research that could prospectively enable industry to attain these objectives' (ibid., p. 1-1).

The construction of the relevance trees was undertaken wholly by Arthur D. Little staff (although comments were later sought from industry), and involved four stages: (i) the identification of significant *industrial objectives* in each sector, the attainment of which would require the application of new technological options; (ii) the identification and description of the relevant *technological options*; (iii) the identification and description of *research approaches* that would lead to these technological options; and (iv) selection from among the *basic research fields* being funded by the NSF of those fields that were judged to be potential sources of scientific knowledge underlying the applied research in each of the six industrial sectors (or those where gaps in basic scientific knowledge were likely to inhibit progress in the applied research leading to the desired technical options). Figure 5.5 provides an example of a 'relevance tree' for the instrumentation industry.

While a full appraisal of this study would require detailed comment from experts in each of the six industrial sectors, a number of general points can be made which perhaps explain why this study, along with the two other discussed below, made little impact within NSF. First, in terms of its operational utility, the 'basic research

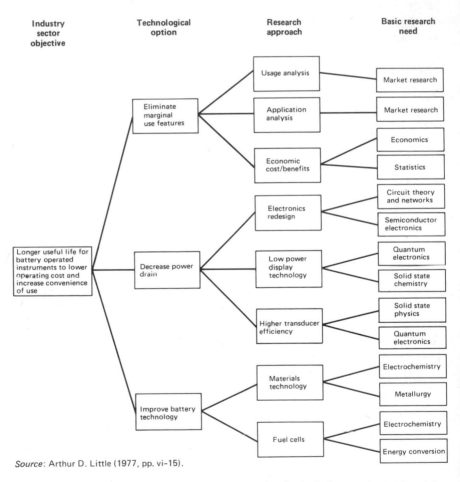

Source: Arthur D. Little (1977, pp. vi-15).

Figure 5.5 Arthur D. Little approach to technological forecasting using relevance trees: example concerning instrumentation industry sector-objective of longer battery life

needs' identified (see the right-hand side of Figure 5.5) tended to be rather general—certainly too general to convince senior scientists who are traditionally sceptical of the role of policy-analysts in helping determine research priorities. Secondly, the failure to involve relevant industrial experts and the basic science community more fully inevitably meant that there was little sense of commitment from these two groups to the results of the study when it was completed.

The task of Battelle in the second study was to analyse the future of science and industry, and the relationship between them, over the decade 1980 to 1990. In consultation with the NSF, five industries were selected for consideration—chemicals, electronics, health-care delivery, metals and transportation—together with the two research areas of chemistry and materials science. The method used in the study is outlined in Figure 5.6, the first step involving the

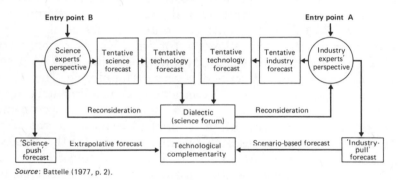

Source: Battelle (1977, p. 2).

Figure 5.6 The Battelle approach to technological forecasting through a dialectic between science and industry perspectives

construction by Battelle of a 'middle-of-the-road' global scenario for the period 1975–2000 to provide a framework for two sets of forecasts. In one of these, five industry experts were asked to imagine they were looking back retrospectively from the year 2000, recording the principal events that had taken place in their industrial sector. On this basis, they attempted to identify the main problems and opportunities that might have confronted the industry, and the technological and scientific advances required to meet them. For the other set of forecasts, four scientific experts were used, two for each research area. Their task was to extrapolate forward from the present to identify 'landmark' scientific events that were expected to occur, the technologies they would generate or support and the industries that would thereby benefit. At a 'science forum', the two sides then discussed their respective 'science-push' and 'industry-pull' forecasts in an effort to reach some agreement on the likely inter-action of science and industry.

The Battelle report (Battelle, 1977), like the Arthur D. Little study, had virtually no impact within NSF. (Those we interviewed in the NSF had mostly either forgotten completely about the studies, or were unaware that they had ever taken place.) The reasons for this are very similar—the failure to involve the academic and indus-trial research communities adequately, and the inability to go beyond very general forecasts. Indeed, several of the predictions made by Battelle subsequently proved rather inaccurate. This was partly because the background scenario given to the experts was itself hopelessly inaccurate, and partly it was the inevitable result of relying on so few experts to make the necessarily wide-ranging industrial and scientific forecasts.

The third study by Technical Audit Associates had a much nar-rower focus, namely electrochemical research and its impact on industry. While this was admittedly only a rather small study (it cost $7,500 which, after allowing for inflation, is roughly com-parable with the cost of the study on which this book is based), its findings can only be described as very disappointing. The twenty-three page report (TAA, 1977) contained (a) a rudimentary survey of existing electrochemical research in universities, government laboratories and industry; (b) three brief case-studies of the effects of basic electrochemical research on industry; and (c) the results of a questionnaire survey of industry. The latter consisted of four questions sent to some twenty firms, thirteen of whom replied. The questions were so bland (for example, 'do you believe that fundamental electrochemical research in this country is adequate?') that it was perhaps inevitable that the report arrived at such anodyne conclusions as the following: 'top-grade electrochemical research is essential for many activities that will affect the future health of the US economy and environment'; 'the linkages between university research and industrial needs are weak'; and (inevitably) 'Federal support of basic electrochemical research is at too low a level' (findings A, D, and E in TAA, 1977, pp. 4–5). About the only con-ceivable benefit of this 'study' is that it may have reassured the NSF that the COSPUP field surveys had not been so unsuccessful after all!

Once these three studies had been completed, they were re-viewed by the NSF task force, which concluded that the metho-dologies employed were not sufficiently advanced to warrant using them as the basis of an improved long-range planning process. Instead, the NSF, in arriving at priorities, continues to rely primarily on the traditional mechanism of expert committees.[11]

5.3 Forecasting in strategic and applied research: the DoE

As noted earlier, several federal agencies are concerned primarily with funding strategic and applied R & D, while also supporting some work of a more fundamental nature. Two of the most important in terms of budgetary size are the Department of Defense (DoD) and the Department of Energy (DoE). We focus on the latter here.

Of the DoE's $4.7 billion R & D budget, some 20 per cent comes under the heading of underlying research for the 'technology base' —for example, high-energy physics, nuclear physics, chemistry, materials science and biological energy. New initiatives in more basic areas are normally left to scientists and are judged by expert committees. Systematic long-term forecasting is not generally seen as appropriate for selecting promising areas of science—optics and lasers were cited by a senior official interviewed as a typical example of a rapid and completely unpredictable development. The overall philosophy of the agency is, on the one hand, to fund a balanced portfolio of research fields likely to yield results of benefit to future development programmes, and, on the other, to support people of merit.

In recent years, however, it has become apparent that one legacy of the rapid expansion of R & D in earlier years is the vast array of expensive research programmes now being supported by DoE. These are generally at the applied and developmental end of the spectrum, and a number have apparently continued with little evident progress for many years. Steps were therefore taken in the early 1980s to reshape the Department's R & D portfolio by identifying programme areas likely to be more *and* less strategically important over the next fifteen to twenty years. Two radically different approaches were adopted.

The first was based upon mathematical forecasting techniques. The aim was to use the SRI/Chase econometric model to predict energy-supply requirements up to the year 2010, and thus construct models of future market-penetration for different energy sources, which in turn could be used to identify areas where R & D was most needed. Some $20,000 was spent on a conceptual study carried out by consultants in association with DoE modellers. However, evaluation of the pilot-study results together with enormous projected costs of the main study led DoE to terminate the work.

Rather greater success was reported as having been achieved with

the second approach. This utilised traditional committee-based procedures for identifying important areas of research, supplemented
with systematic techniques for judging priorities. The work was
carried out by the Energy Research Advisory Board (ERAB), the
main external advisory group to the DoE, as part of a wider study
of R & D priorities. Most of ERAB's efforts were directed towards
the DoE's applied programme (particularly interesting debates took
place on the programmes relating to electric vehicles, synthetic
fuels and breeder-reactor demonstrations, for example). However,
we shall concentrate here on their analysis of more basic research—
the so-called 'technology-base programmes'. (Further details of
ERAB's conclusions can be found in DoE, 1981.)

ERAB began by agreeing upon a set of criteria to prioritise DoE
basic-research programmes. These included scientific potential,
inventive potential, mission impact, urgency and federal R & D role.
A modified Delphi procedure was then employed in which the
twenty-two ERAB members (including nine industrialists) (i) assessed
the relative importance they attached to the various criteria, and
(ii) evaluated each programme area in terms of them. By combining
the two sets of results, overall figures for the respective merit of
each programme area were obtained. Histograms of voting profiles
for the different programme areas were also produced, and, where
major differences of opinion existed, these were discussed by ERAB.
(In 50 per cent of cases, however, the histograms revealed such
a level of consensus that no further discussion was necessary.) Two
interesting innovations were adopted in this second phase: the
committee debates were held in public—to keep them 'honest',
as one interviewee put it; and, in areas of particular disagreement,
an 'opponent' and 'proponent' were appointed to stimulate discussion, the debate continuing until a measure of agreement was
reached (apart from two cases where minority reports had to be
submitted). Overall, DoE considers this to have been an interesting
experiment, although not a completely successful one. While some
degree of rank-ordering in basic research categories emerged (and
certain broad fields of research such as materials science subsequently
benefited from increased support), the results were judged to have
been insufficiently discriminating to be operationally very useful.
However, the ERAB report did succeed in generating considerable
debate and received widespread media coverage, opening up the
process of setting priorities for R & D and leading within a comparatively short period to hearings on Capitol Hill on the report's
findings. One senior DoE official gave the following assessment:

The net result of the ensuing debate between the Administration and Congress was a budget remarkably in line with the ERAB priority and funding recommendations . . . The extent to which the ERAB study was responsible for the final outcome is, of course, unclear. What can be said with some certainty is that the ERAB process provided a mechanism for sorting out the contending and conflicting views, and a public forum in which the basic arguments could be exposed, rationally and objectively. [Snow, 1983, p. 9.]

5.4 Overall research forecasting: OSTP

Although the US scientific community and federal agencies have long supported the doctrine of pluralism in funding, and the associated decentralisation in decision-making over priorities, pressures on the overall science budget eventually led to demands, particularly from Congress, for greater co-ordination and prioritisation. Steps to develop a more coherent overall government policy towards R & D were therefore taken in the mid-1970s with the creation of the Office of Science and Technology Policy (OSTP) within the President's Executive Office.

According to the 1976 Act on 'Science and Technology Policy, Organization and Priorities', the role of OSTP was to assist the Executive Branch in improving policy-making in science and technology, and in particular to 'identify and assess emerging and future areas in which science and technology can be used effectively in addressing national and international problems' (US Congress, 1976, section 205).[12] Among its responsibilities, OSTP was required to prepare each year a *Five-Year Outlook on Science and Technology* and an *Annual Science and Technology Report*. However, after some re-organisation in 1977 by the new Carter Administration, it became clear that OSTP did not have the resources (nor, in the view of some, the inclination), to fulfil all its functions. Responsibility for preparing the two reports was therefore transferred to the National Science Foundation. Since OSTP was (and still is) the only body in a position to prepare an overview of all R & D areas, this was clearly likely to result in problems. As one NSF official commented:

To have expected NSF—a relatively small line agency with responsibility primarily for basic research in universities to have convinced the heads of all the other R & D agencies to lay out their options, then to have convinced the Director of OSTP to convince the President to present, to the Congress, those options along with his own priorities was totally unrealistic. [Private correspondence, 1984.]

It is therefore hardly surprising that the transfer of responsibility from OSTP to NSF soon gave rise to certain problems.[13]

The procedure adopted by the NSF[14] in preparing the first two *Five-Year Outlooks*[15] was to solicit contributions from the National Academy of Sciences, federal agencies and individual experts. These were analysed and synthesised by the NSF, and published together with an edited collection of the main submissions. However, it was not long before the first *Outlook* (NSF, 1980b), and, to a lesser extent, the second (NSF, 1982b) were subject to criticisms very similar to those levelled at the NAS field surveys. In particular, they were regarded as being over-long and academic;[16] they tended to be discipline-based, rather than focusing on technological, industrial and social problems; there was little analysis of the likely longer-term economic significance of different research areas; and absolutely no attempt was made to establish priorities (cf. Blanpied and Leshner, 1981, p. 148). In short, the NSF was widely seen as having adopted too passive and uncritical a stance towards the material submitted, and as having failed to introduce a genuine strategic overview. Although attempts were made to exercise more direction in the second *Outlook*, this too was criticised by several of those interviewed (particularly in the General Accounting Office and Office of Management and Budget) for failing to address the interests of either Congress or the Executive (it tended to assume a scientific audience). More seriously, it was dismissed as operationally worthless by NSF officials.

By no means can all the blame for this state of affairs be attached to the NSF. If the *Outlook* was intended to constitute a five-year forecast for science and technology, then, in view of the diversity of funding mechanisms in the US, it was clearly unrealistic to expect one agency (particularly that with the most fundamental orientation and the least connected to industry) to prepare an overview. OSTP was consequently criticised for having abdicated responsibility for preparing the *Outlook* (cf. ibid., pp. 152–3). Yet, when these problems became apparent, rather than restoring responsibility for the *Outlook* back to OSTP, as many advocated, it was instead subcontracted by the NSF in 1982 to the Committee on Science, Engineering, and Public Policy[17]—in other words, closer to the scientific community and even further away from policy-makers. Hardly surprisingly, therefore, we found little evidence that the third *Outlook* (COSEPUP, 1982) was any more useful to policy-makers. It too appeared to suffer from many of the failings of the field surveys, in particular the reluctance of researchers to discuss— let alone decide upon—priorities between different scientific areas.

This perhaps explains the recent decision by Congress to abolish the requirement for a separate *Outlook*. Instead, Congress has specified that one chapter in the *Annual Science and Technology Report* (required 'not less than biennially') be devoted to an assessment of future trends and opportunities, together with their social and economic implications.

By the first year of the Reagan Administration, strong criticism of the *Outlooks* and more generally of the state of long-range research planning in the United States had begun to be voiced publicly (see, for example, Staats, 1980, and GAO, 1981). Since then, George Keyworth, Science Adviser to the President and Director of OSTP, has launched several initiatives aimed at improving procedures for setting overall R & D priorities. While accepting that the diversity of US research-funding mechanisms has generally ensured that good scientists have been able to obtain support, Keyworth argues that it has also led to proliferation of mediocre research and to duplication of effort (see Barfield, 1982, pp. 42–9). With the country facing a growing technological challenge from overseas, particularly from Japan, this somewhat inefficient approach, he argues, can no longer be afforded. Even if the science budget continues to expand as rapidly over coming years as it did between 1980 and 1984,[18] there is still likely to be a need for considerably greater central co-ordination and strategic thinking. Keyworth recognises that such a re-orientation can only be imposed by an OSTP better integrated into the policy-making process, and that the scientific community may be reluctant to co-operate. Currently, OSTP is trying to persuade funding agencies to take prioritisation and strategic thinking more seriously, but, if this proves unsuccessful, priorities may eventually have to be imposed from above.[19]

The most significant result of Keyworth's intervention has been the establishment of a series of 'Research Briefings' undertaken jointly by the National Academies of Science and Engineering, and the Institute of Medicine. The two aims were to identify research areas likely to yield high future dividends, and to provide a new channel of communication between the federal government and the scientific community. The process was described by some of the officials interviewed as having been somewhat *ad hoc*, even circular, in the sense that in order to be chosen as the subject of a Research Briefing a field had first to be identified in some way as a 'priority' area. Keyworth began by asking the NAS President to help set priorities among fields of science, but NAS apparently refused, arguing that this was the role of OSTP. They did agree to identify (but not prioritise) areas of particular scientific opportunity within specific fields of science, a proposal which Keyworth accepted. Over thirty fields were identified for consideration in the initial round of briefings, and discussions between the NAS and Keyworth subsequently narrowed these down to seven.

The actual task of reviewing the seven areas was entrusted to COSEPUP, who set up panels of about a dozen experts to prepare each briefing. Significantly, these panels had a much broader membership than the survey committees in early COSPUP studies, including some young scientists and a greater proportion of industrial representatives. They met for two or three days, analysing submissions from the academic research community, government and industry. Draft reports were prepared, circulated for comment, and revised. The panel's chairman then made a one-hour presentation first to COSEPUP and later to Keyworth and his staff.[20] This exercise was repeated in 1983 with another five areas (this time selected by COSEPUP and subsequently ratified by Keyworth).

From our interviews, it would appear that the Research Briefings have had some impact on policy-making.[21] They have also focused attention on the quality of US research with concern being expressed that some is mediocre.[22] Nevertheless, they have apparently not escaped the familiar failings of previous attempts by the scientific community at research forecasting. Often, they have tended to be more a review of *existing* opportunities—a 'wish-list', as one official put it—than a systematic attempt to look at the longer-term future. The fields on which the briefings focused were, as we have seen, selected in advance in a not particularly rigorous fashion. Lastly, according to certain interviewees, this latest initiative has once again been 'captured' by the scientific community, who have been able to obtain agreement to produce field surveys under another guise— in other words, reviews that concentrate on the likely *scientific* impact of particular research areas, without considering the possible technological and economic effects, thereby excluding any possibility of establishing priorities and an overall strategy. From the point of view of the present study, they illustrate once more the dangers of devolving responsibility for the selection of promising areas of science largely to the basic research community.

5.5 Research forecasting: science-based firms

The three firms visited in the American part of this study all emphasised the growing importance of strategic research for their business activities. This reflects the substantial growth in industrial R & D within the US since the start of the 1980s. For example, between 1981 and 1982, industrially financed R & D grew by 7 per cent in real terms (to $40 billion), the greatest increase being in the chemical sector where the real growth-rate was nearer 12 per cent. As a result, the ratio of total US expenditure on R & D (by industry and government) divided by net sales jumped from 3.1 per cent in 1981 to 3.6 per cent in 1982, the largest annual change ever recorded during the last twenty-five years (cf. NSF, 1984, p. 1).

Given this background trend, the situation of Company E (a large electrical and electronics manufacturer) is probably not untypical. The company currently invests just under 7 per cent of sales on R & D, one-seventh being spent on the corporate R & D division, which is responsible for the firm's longer-term strategic research. Between 1981 and 1982, the resources devoted to 'long-range futures' research were dramatically increased by over 20 per cent, with a major expansion in corporate R & D, including the construction of new laboratories for advanced electronics and micro-electronics at a cost of over $100 million. Yet as recently as 1977 the position of the company was very different. In that year, worries that the company had not been investing enough in R & D and was therefore insufficiently technologically orientated relative to its international competitors—and in particular that it had almost 'missed the boat' in relation to micro-electronics—resulted in the setting up of a major technological forecasting exercise. This was undertaken by a high-level corporate team. The aim was to predict future technological trends and the associated market opportunities, the forces driving these changes, their effects on the company and its ability to mount an effective response. After reviewing the literature and assessing previous forecasts, the committee selected various technologies of potential importance to the company (such as bio-engineering and micro-electronic control systems). Forecasts for each technology were then prepared by sub-panels of well regarded R & D staff drawn from the corporate R & D laboratory and various divisions. In particular, the sub-panels attempted to identify what were termed emerging 'research phase areas' (where more basic research was still needed to yield viable products—for example, in voice-identification). Finally, the forecasts were reviewed by senior staff in the company.

Views on the value of the exercise were mixed. True, it reconfirmed the importance of electronics to the company's future. It was also a valuable experience for those involved; the process of bringing together staff from throughout the company to interact creatively was widely seen as beneficial. On the other hand, the forecasts cost several million dollars, while the dozen weighty volumes they yielded have apparently not had much impact on corporate policy, perhaps because they identified little that was not already known. Overall, therefore, the forecasting exercise was not generally regarded by those interviewed in the company as having been particularly successful. One result is that a centralised approach to research forecasting (at least at the programme level) has been dropped by the company.

Despite this disappointing experience, Company E has, as noted earlier, substantially increased the emphasis given to longer-term research over recent years. At the corporate R & D laboratory, the procedure now used is to set annual cash limits for individual broad areas of R & D, using the process outlined in Figure 5.7. Detailed research priorities are then drawn up at a departmental level. Longer-term research questions are dealt with by (a) ensuring that newly recruited staff are of a high calibre and possess expertise specific to areas likely to be important in the future (such as knowledge-engineering or metal substitutes), and (b) setting aside 10 per cent of the R & D budget for less focused research, on the assumption that this can sometimes lead to beneficial results (for example, research on superconductivity was later useful in NMR equipment).[23]

The experience of Company F (one of the world's leading forces in computers and information technology) with formal forecasting has also not been entirely satisfactory, and a decision was taken a few years ago to disband its well known in-house futurological group (it had been responsible for the development of the 'consensor' described in note 25 below). The company spends the equivalent of around 6.5 per cent of sales on research and development, corporate research (or 'science') accounting for 10 per cent of the total. However, given that some of the activities formally classified as 'development' include basic technology programmes, the proportion of funds devoted to longer-term research is actually between 15 and 20 per cent of the R & D budget. This is in line with Company F's belief in the need for a vigorous science programme free from any specific economic objectives. The purpose is to provide a 'window' on the outside scientific world (in particular, through personal contacts and conferences) so that surprising but potentially important advances, especially those arising in academic research, can be promptly recognised. Current corporate research interests include cognition and artificial intelligence, ceramics, polymers and surface chemistry. The main criterion used in initiating new lines of research is that the work must be of world quality, and this generally means putting together a team of at least a dozen scientists. Competitive internal peer review is an important element in the project-selection process.

The identification of R & D opportunities starts each year with an evaluation of progress and momentum in forefront technologies applicable to business opportunities and an analysis of corporate strengths and weaknesses in these technologies, resulting in an urgency ranking of strategic technology areas.

o Among the inputs are:

 – Technology implications cf corporate strategy
 – Sector and in-house technology needs and opportunities
 – Outlook for and rate of progress in major technology areas: innovative ideas and leapfrog technologies
 – Recent progress in ongoing corporate programs
 – Strategies and goals of competitors

o 1983 Urgency Ranking of Technology Areas

 A – Advanced electronics
 U – Productivity and automation
 R – Information, communication, and control
 G – Plastics and silicones
 E – Metals and ceramics
 N – Energy conservation and use
 C – Energy conversion and delivery
 Y – New or defensive programs

'Urgency' is determined by:

o Market pull – how important to company E

o Technology push – rate of advance in the technology

o Competition – actual competitive position of company E compared to what it should be

Other corporate R & D activities of high urgency are those aimed at resolving sudden crises or exploiting unique opportunities.

Source: Material supplied by Company E.

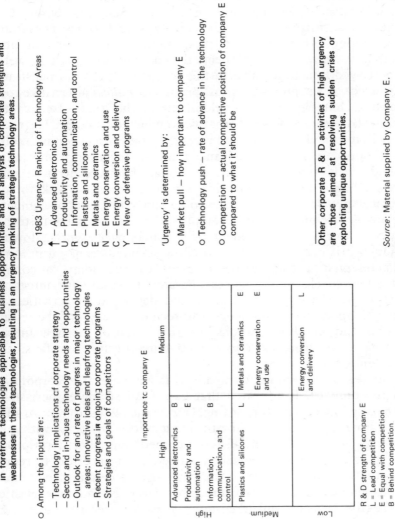

Importance to company E

Rate of advance	High	Medium
High	Advanced electronics — B; Productivity and automation — E; Information, communication, and control — B	
Medium	Plastics and silicones — L	Metals and ceramics — E; Energy conservation and use — E
Low		Energy conversion and delivery — L

R & D strength of company E
L = Lead competition
E = Equal with competition
B = Behind competition

Figure 5.7 Strategy development for R & D by Company E

The Corporate Technical Committee (consisting of the Company Chief Scientist and six members appointed on a one-year full-time assignment to corporate headquarters) has the role of 'influencing the long-term scientific and technical direction of the enterprise and its overall well-being'. It is aided by a Science Advisory Committee of distinguished outside scientists and other consultants, who, among other responsibilities, review existing and proposed research in terms of its intellectual and scientific merit as well as its perceived long-term value to the company.[24] The normal strategy is to select and support the most promising *radical* alternative to the known technology under development at the time—for example, optical data-storage as an alternative to magnetic storage. The radical alternative can change, as it did recently when Josephson technology was dropped in favour of advanced silicon technology and gallium arsenide after tens of millions of dollars had already been spent. When a major decision like this has to be made, a task force of technical people is often convened to study the risks of competing options—weighing up, for example, whether a success in technology x is worth the investment of y dollars over z years. However, although it is corporate policy to allow scientists engaged in longer-term research a considerable element of autonomy, a complex system of checks and balances operates to ensure the integration of their work with more applied and development activities. For example, operating divisions regularly review the work of the research division and make suggestions for the initiation of new lines of research, while plans exist to second temporarily scientific staff to development divisions.

The Textile Division of Company G (a large chemical corporation) was the only US firm visited that expressed strong enthusiasm for systematic longer-term forecasting. During the 1970s, it took on all the well known characteristics of a firm in a mature industry, with much emphasis being placed on cost-containment and short-term profits. Long-range research consequently suffered. In an effort to remedy the situation, and to react to the challenge of certain newly emerging technologies (such as composite materials and new plastics), the Textile Division embarked upon a major forecasting exercise in 1981. This had two components. The first, entitled 'A view of the year 2000', focused on future social and economic needs and on how the resources of the textile industry might be mobilised to meet them. In other words, it took a 'market-pull' approach, while the second, in contrast, concentrated on 'science-push' possibilities. The study, which cost over $1 million and involved six person-years of effort, employed a variety of techniques including (i) a

survey of the research literature on social, economic and technological trends, (ii) a patent search (to identify new or rapidly growing
technologies and the innovating organisations), (iii) citation analysis
(to identify experts in different scientific fields), (iv) scenario analysis
(and cross-impact analysis) and (v) extensive group discussions (among
company staff and consultants, specially invited academics, and
professional forecasters) making use of a 'consensor'.[25]

In contrast to Firm E, forecasts within the Textile Division of
Company G appear to have had a considerable impact on corporate
R & D policy. A number of possible reasons can be identified. First,
whereas the forecasting exercise undertaken by Firm E focused
on the likely paths of development for particular technologies,
Company G's approach reflected a clearer understanding of the
innovation process—that innovations represent a *coupling* of science
or technology 'push' with market 'pull'. Secondly, the interaction
of Company G's research and managerial staff with professional
forecasters and outside experts proved very productive. Thirdly,
there appears to have been a more receptive attitude towards the
forecasts among corporate senior management. This was because
the need for more long-range research had been recognised before
the exercise began, the only question being *which* areas of research
should be chosen. The results were therefore readily accepted and
implemented; within a year, nearly a quarter of the Textile Division's
longer-term R & D had been redirected. Finally, Company G's
product-lines depend upon a much narrower range of technology
than those of Company E which needs to keep track of large numbers of new technologies in making generally incremental innovations
to existing products. In contrast, Company G can achieve success
with a few radical product innovations (such as new construction
materials) as long as it is able to develop appropriate process technology. Since the time-horizon to full-scale production may be more
than ten years into the future, this makes the need for longer-term
forecasting all the greater.

5.6 Research forecasting: consultancies

Since US consultancy organisations have often played a central role
in undertaking studies of strategically important areas of research
for both government and industry, they are well placed to comment
on the 'state-of-the-art' in this field, and a number were therefore
visited in the course of our study. Of these, Computer Horizons
Incorporated (CHI Research) is engaged in activities of potentially
the greatest relevance to research forecasting. Over recent years, CHI

has developed a unique data-bank on US patenting activity, including that by foreign firms. In addition to all the information normally held in patent data-banks—on innovating firms, characteristics of the innovations and so on—CHI includes the references contained in the patents both to previous relevant patents, and to the research literature on which the patent-application is based. By examining the interrelation of heavily 'cited' patents, one can construct 'maps' of technological domains, and assess the relative positions of different companies (or countries) within the domain. Such knowledge is generally sold to firms for use in strategic research planning (see, in particular, Carpenter et al., 1981; Narin, 1983; Narin et al., 1983), enabling them to keep track of 'hot' technological frontier areas.

Similar analyses can also be carried out relating patents to earlier basic research. It is possible, for example, to identify for given patent classes the areas and types of research providing important inputs to patent applications. For example, in the case of 38,300 US patents registered between 1975 and 1980, some 40 per cent of the citations to scientific research were to chemistry, while physics accounted for just 13 per cent (Carpenter, 1983, p. 24). Certain industrial sectors are also clearly more dependent on science than others. One recent (and as yet unpublished) study found that defence-related companies are more than twice as dependent on the scientific literature as other firms, and that they rely particularly on applied physics, electronics, and solid-state physics (interview, 1983).

CHI Research has also found that many patents cite surprisingly recent research articles: the average age of cited papers is around five years, but it is considerably less in areas like electronics and biochemistry (cf. Carpenter and Narin, 1978; Carpenter et al., 1981). One possibility is that national science-planners could therefore analyse recent patents (say, over the previous twelve months) to identify which areas of basic research have in the past few years yielded most patentable ideas. Moreover, by monitoring the citation characteristics of patents over time, one could establish which research areas are increasing or decreasing in importance. In particular, those fields of science contributing to rapidly developing technologies (where there is likely to be only a short delay of one to three years between the publication of research and subsequent patenting) could be identified at a relatively early stage, perhaps permitting decisions to be taken by government about investing resources in time for benefits to be derived from the newly emerging technologies. The inherent disadvantage of the approach is the cost of computing required to generate the comprehensive research profiles needed by governments. There is also a distinct possibility that this new research-planning technique may affect future corporate publishing practices or even the references cited in patents.

Another consultancy company that has been attempting to develop a new approach to scientific planning is the Center for Research Planning (CRP). CRP has signed a joint-venture agreement with the Institute for Scientific Information (ISI) to exploit the latter's publication and citation data base for policy purposes. Each year, ISI scans half a million papers in some 3,000 of the world's leading scientific journals (although the coverage is highly uneven across non-English language countries). For each paper, the references to previous research articles are abstracted and recorded on computer. Of the three main sections to the *Science Citation Index* (published annually by ISI), one lists by author all papers published that year in the journals scanned, while a second lists the papers by institutional affiliation of their first-named authors. Counting its publications provides a means by which to obtain some indication of the scientific output of a particular research group, university or laboratory .

It is, however, the third section of the *Science Citation Index* which has the greatest potential for policy purposes. This lists all the articles cited by the 500,000 papers published and scanned that year. One can therefore establish for individual papers the scientists who have referred to them during the year, and the total number of times they have been cited. If one assumes that the authors of scientific papers are, through the act of referring to other articles, acknowledging some form of intellectual link between their papers and the cited articles, then citation analysis can be used to determine which research papers (or scientists or laboratories) have had most impact on the work of other scientists in a given year.[26]

An alternative approach, termed 'co-citation' analysis, starts from a slightly different assumption that, if two articles are both referred to, or 'co-cited', by the paper, then this also implies the existence of an intellectual link between them. It is further assumed that the more frequently two articles are co-cited by other papers, the stronger are the links. By identifying the most frequently co-cited papers in a particular research field, and 'mapping' them (using computerised clustering techniques) according to their frequency of co-citation (i.e. the papers that are most frequently co-cited are placed nearest to each other in the research map drawn, and vice versa), it is claimed that one can produce a 'model' of the intellectual structure of the field concerned. (A map for fracture mechanics of ceramics and glass is shown in Figure 5.8.) Furthermore,

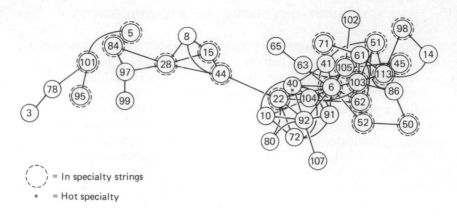

```
(  )  = In specialty strings

 *    = Hot specialty
```

Specialty No.	Specialty Name	Specialty No.	Specialty Name
3	Properties of lithium nitride	63	Erosion of silicon single-crystals
5	Beta-alumina ceramics: deterioration (String #28)	65	Influence of microstructure on the erosion of ductile solids
6	Identation techniques for measuring fracture toughness (String #3)	71	Transformation toughening in ceramics (String #23)
8	Creep-behaviour of ceramics	72	Phase equilibria of silicon aluminium oxynitrides
10	Role of various elements and compounds in the nitriding of silicon	78	Ionic properties of zirconium phosphates
14	Stress intensity factors	80	Sintering and high-temperature properties of Si_3N_4 and SiC
15	Thermal-activation of dislocations (String #38)	84	MgO additions and microstructural properties (String #33)
22	Composition and densification kinetics of hot-pressed silicon nitride (String #3)	86	Metallic dispersions and fibres in glasses
28	High temperature plastic deformation and conductivity in Al_2O_3 (String #30)	91	Crystal growth and structure
		92	Sintering and hot-pressing
40	Silicon-nitride materials and the composition of polytype alloys	95	Effects of air and water exposure on aluminas (String #13)
41	Properties of mullite-zirconia composites and silicon-nitride ceramics	97	Grain-boundary diffusion
		98	Fracturing and crack growth (String #27)
44	High-temperature creep-behaviour of chain boundaries (String #11)	99	Effects of space-charge and grain-boundary segregation on conductivity of crystals
45	Fracture-mechanics of ceramics (String #27)	101	Beta-alumina films (String #28)
50	Fracture-toughness tests of ceramics (String #24)	102	Strengths of optical glass fibres
51	Spontaneous and stress-induced microcracking in glass (String #23)	103	Measurement of thermal diffusivity in ceramics (String #22)
		104	Thermal diffusivity of silicon-nitride
52	Statistical evaluation of fatigue experiments and proof testing in ceramics (String #31)	105	Contact damage resistance of glasses (String #3)
61	Grain-size dependence of fracture energy	107	Oxynitride glasses and glass ceramics
62	Double-torsion fracture-mechanics (String #9)	113	Measurement of stresses and fractures in ceramics (String #27)

Source: Material supplied by Center for Research Planning, Philadelphia.

Figure 5.8 A co-citation map for fracture mechanics of ceramics and glass

by comparing the cognitive map for one year with that for subsequent years, one can perhaps identify rapidly changing research areas within a field.[27]

The Center for Research Planning has carried out a number of studies for government agencies and research foundations, producing 'models' of various research areas by clustering highly cocited papers. By using experts to interpret the resulting maps of 'research domains', CRP believes that it can identify newly emerging areas of research and the most active institutions in a domain (CRP, 1983). This approach may have some potential value for the planning of basic research, although the costs involved are by no means negligible because of the huge volume of data analysis involved. One major problem, however, is that the ISI data base is biased towards areas of fundamental science. The CRP approach may therefore prove less successful for more strategic or applied areas of science. Moreover, it can clearly only provide information from a 'science-push' viewpoint.

As for other consultancy organisations, Battelle and SRI International appear to have done little of direct relevance for strategic research planning (apart from the Battelle studies for NSF discussed earlier). They have been mainly concerned with examining the prospects for *given* technologies and predicting future markets, rather than identifying areas of strategic research likely to have a major technological impact. However, the conditions of confidentiality imposed by their clients meant that we were unable to examine the work of these organisations fully.

The same is true of the Institute for the Future, which has carried out work for many companies on identifying market and technological opportunities. However, as we saw in connection with Company G, the Institute has also looked at questions of strategic research planning. Indeed, it claims to be a leader in the development and application of rigorous forecasting methods (such as Delphi techniques) to corporate decision-making. Its approach is based on systematically identifying the experts for the field concerned, obtaining and weighting their views according to their competence, and using a two- or three-stage iterative procedure to arrive at the final results. When such an approach is properly integrated into a forecasting exercise co-ordinated by policy-makers and the research community concerned, such systematic procedures may be of considerable value. Certainly, the experiences of Company G (assuming that they are not untypical) would suggest that the approach merits attention in any attempt to introduce greater systematisation into expert-committee determinations of future research priorities.

Overall, we have seen in this chapter how the United States' attempts to identify basic research areas of longer-term promise have met with a mixed response. The NSF and NAS have experimented with a variety of methods. The approach based on field surveys carried out by panels of distinguished researchers was (at least in the early COSPUP surveys) not very systematic, and it generally failed to establish which of the competing areas of scientific opportunity should be given priority. However, the subsequent attempt by the NSF to employ professional forecasters and formal forecasting techniques fared no better, and since then it has reverted to more traditional approaches. The DoE's experiences with professional forecasters proved similarly unproductive. Rather greater success was, however, achieved with the ERAB exercise where a panel in which industry was well represented adopted a fairly systematic approach to establishing R & D priorities for the DoE. As for overall research forecasting, OSTP's experience with the *Five-Year Outlooks* was not particularly satisfactory. The *Outlooks* suffered from many of the same inadequacies as the COSPUP field surveys, in particular the failure to give sufficient attention to likely economic and technological benefits and the inability to provide a strategic overview. In the more recent 'Research Briefings', despite a greater attempt having been made to involve industrial researchers, the reports have once again tended to be dominated by 'science-push' considerations.

In industry, experiences have also been mixed, with Companies E and F having experimented with more formal approaches to longer-term forecasting and rejected them. Company G, in contrast, has had rather greater success perhaps because of the combination of (i) integrating both 'science-push' and 'demand-pull' perspectives in forecasting, (ii) achieving a fruitful interaction between forecasters and researchers, and (iii) a receptive attitude towards the forecasts on the part of senior management. The final section then described how certain US consultancy companies, in particular CHI Research, have begun to develop techniques of potential interest to those concerned with identifying important new areas of basic research. We now move on to consider Japan where, as we shall see, far more effort has been devoted to long-term foresight activities and considerably greater success has apparently been achieved.

Notes

1. The National Institutes of Health (NIH), which is by far the largest supporter of basic research in the US (spending about $1.9 billion on it in 1982),

represents a combination of categories (i) and (ii). It is a mission-orientated agency like DoE and DoD, except that research is primarily done by universities rather than industry. There was unfortunately insufficient time in our study to visit NIH, or DoD, the next largest supporter of basic research after NSF. (NSF spent nearly $1 billion in the 1982 fiscal year, compared with just over $0.7 billion by DoD, and slightly less by DoE—see NSF, 1982a, p. 38, table 28.)

2. Evidence to support this argument comes, for example, from TRACES (IIT Research Institute, 1968)—see Chapter 2. For a recent formulation of this view, see NSF (1979, and 1980a).

3. As at other basic-research foundations, senior officials found it hard to justify the prevailing balance of expenditure between fields.

4. As noted earlier, a description of NAS can be found in Ronayne (1984, pp. 109-11).

5. One of the few who attempted to address the question of what criteria should be employed in choosing between scientific fields was Dr A. M. Weinberg (1963). While his suggested criteria generated considerable discussion (see Shils, 1968), the operational influence that they had on policy-making is debatable.

6. As one senior government official interviewed explained, 'it was difficult to sift the substance from the rhetoric'. (Interview, 1983.)

7. This neglect by the Westheimer Report of the industrial significance of chemistry was one reason why a study on 'Chemistry and the Economy' was subsequently undertaken. Yet, although this exhaustively documented the impact of chemistry on industry in the past, it did not attempt to establish future research priorities. It consequently had little impact on policy-making, being dismissed by some as just another exercise in special pleading.

8. In forwarding the Pake Report on Physics to the National Academy of Sciences, the COSPUP Chairman noted that 'no attempt has been made to identify relative priorities of the various fiscal needs in case that total budget does not grow at the recommended rate [of 21 per cent per annum].' (Pake, 1965, forwarding letter by G. B. Kistiakowsky.) Similar criticisms were also levelled by COSPUP at the Greenstein Report on Astronomy. It is significant that the report of the most recent NAS Astronomy Survey Committee (Field, 1982), which does establish clear priorities for the field, is much more favourably regarded by government officials. (The fact that it is also less than 200 pages long is also seen as a significant advantage.)

9. The comments of this senior government official were not untypical: 'The scientific community and especially NAS [the National Academy of Sciences] lost a lot of public credibility with its future surveys. They did not and still do not make a good job with priorities at all. And they do not try to pick out dying areas. They just point out growth areas and demand more money. The public has got fed up about it.' (Interview, 1983.)

10. The remaining committee member was a government official.

11. We have not considered in this section the significant effort on the part of

the NSF in producing material on the status of, and trends in, particular scientific areas. Most important is the biennial *Science Indicators*—by far the best national compilation of R & D statistics. Over the period 1981–83, the NSF also published an annual volume on *Emerging Issues in Science and Technology* outlining general science-policy questions, but this has now been discontinued. Finally, NSF produces annual *Status of Science Reviews* for 'limited distribution for internal use only'. These give an extremely useful overview of the state of NSF activities on a programme-by-programme basis.

12. A detailed description of OSTP's functions can be found in Ronayne (1984, pp. 106–9).

13. OSTP was later criticised by the General Accounting Office for having neglected key aspects of its legislative mandate concerning federal research priorities (Comptroller General of the United States, 1980). There is an interesting discussion of the problems leading to the transfer of responsibility for the two reports to the NSF in US House of Representatives (1979). A more general critique of US long-term scientific planning can be found in Staats (1980).

14. This section draws heavily on an excellent review of the origins and aims of the *Five-Year Outlook* by Blanpied and Leshner (1981), as well as other contributions to Chubin and Rossini (1981).

15. We focus here on this rather than the *Annual Science and Technology Report* because of its longer-term horizon.

16. The first at least was also rather expensive, costing about $1 million.

17. COSEPUP is a joint committee of the National Academy of Sciences, the National Academy of Engineering, and the Institute of Medicine. It is the descendant of the NAS Committee, COSPUP.

18. See Keyworth (1984) for a review of trends in government support of R & D over this period. A useful discussion of the background to science policy under the Reagan Administration is given in Barfield (1982).

19. Scientists' arguments that prioritisation is impossible now seem rather hollow given that researchers *have* been able in certain isolated cases (such as materials science, as we saw in section 5.2) to agree upon priorities, although usually only when forced to by shortage of funds.

20. Subsequently, the briefings were also given to the Director and senior management of NSF, and to other federal departments and agencies. They are published collectively in COSEPUP (1983).

21. For example, the impact of the Research Briefing on astronomy was reported to be a major reason why the Astronomy Division of NSF received a 25 per cent budget increase in Fiscal Year 1984. This raises the question, however, of whether the big sciences are, as in the COSPUP field surveys, inevitably at an advantage over less well organised, more diffuse small sciences.

22. In the case of one of the Research Briefings reported as having been poorly received, this was taken by OSTP to indicate that the particular area was bereft of new ideas.

23. In 1982 a new committee was set up to decide upon the funding of promising research areas within the corporate R & D laboratory. Its annual budget was $500,000, which supported four or five programmes. Proposals selected had to (a) be in important research areas for the company's future, (b) result in publishable work, and (c) involve young scientists. This experiment was terminated, however, after one year.
24. The main features of Company F's approach to determining R & D strategy are outlined in Branscomb (1982, and 1983).
25. The consensor is used to weight the judgements of participants in a Delphi exercise according to their relative competence, and to produce (in real time) aggregate judgements while maintaining individual confidentiality.
26. See, for example, Martin and Irvine (1983) for a detailed discussion of citation analysis, its limitations and how these may be overcome.
27. Further description of co-citation analysis and of its relevance to strategic planning can be found in the useful summary article by Rothman (1984). An example of how it may be used to identify national strengths and weaknesses in R & D performance is contained in Mombers et al. (1984). More recently, a group at the Centre de Sociologie de l'Innovation in Paris has developed an alternative approach known as 'co-word analysis', which is based upon the key words employed in abstracting and indexing scientific papers. The approach is summarised in ibid., while a more detailed description is given in Callon et al. (1983).

References

Barfield, C. E. (1982), *Science Policy from Ford to Reagan*, Washington, D.C., American Enterprise Institute for Public Policy Research.

Battelle (1977), *Forecasting Science and Industry*, report prepared for the Office of Planning and Policy Analysis of the National Science Foundation, Washington, D.C., Battelle Columbus Laboratories.

Bers, L. (1968), *The Mathematical Sciences: A Report*, report by the Bers Committee to the National Academy of Sciences, Washington, D.C., National Academy of Sciences.

Blanpied, W. A. and Leshner, A. I. (1981), 'Origins and aims of the Five-Year Outlook', *Technological Forecasting and Social Change* 20, pp. 145–54.

Branscomb, L. M. (1982), 'Industry evaluation of research quality: edited excerpts from a seminar', *Science, Technology and Human Values* 7(39), pp. 15–22.

Branscomb, L. M. (1983), 'Corporate direction and R & D', paper presented at 'Conference on R & D: Key Issues for Management', New York, 20 April, mimeo, Armonk, N.J., IBM.

Bromley, D. A. (1972), *Physics in Perspective*, report by the Bromley Committee to the National Academy of Sciences, Washington, D.C., National Academy of Sciences.

Callon, M., Courtial, J-P., Turner, W. A. and Bauin, S. (1983), 'From translations to problematic networks: an introduction to co-word analysis', *Social Science Information*, 22, pp. 191–235.

Carpenter, M. P. (1983), 'Patent citations as indicators of scientific and technological linkages', paper presented to AAAS Annual Meeting, Detroit, Michigan, 30 May, mimeo, Cherry Hill, N.J., CHI Research.

Carpenter, M. P. and Narin, F. (1978), *Utilization of Scientific Literature by U.S. Patents*, report to NSF (PRM–7801694 CHI 782–R), mimeo, Cherry Hill, N.J., CHI Research.

Carpenter, M. P., Narin, F. and Woolff, P. (1981), 'Citation rates to technologically important patents', *World Patent Information* 3(4), pp. 160–3.

Chubin, D. E. and Rossini, F. A. (eds) (1981), *Special Issue of 'Technological Forecasting and Social Change': The Five-Year Outlook on Science and Technology in the United States*, New York, Elsevier.

Cohen, M. (1974), *Materials and Man's Needs*, report by the Cohen Committee to the National Academy of Sciences, Washington, D.C., National Academy of Sciences.

Comptroller General of the US (1980), *The Office of Science and Technology Policy: Adaptation to a President's Operating Style May Conflict with Congressionally Mandated Assignments* (GAO Report PAD–80–79), Washington, D.C., General Accounting Office.

COSEPUP (1982), *The Outlook for Science and Technology: The Next Five Years*, a report by the Committee on Science, Engineering and Public Policy for the NSF, Washington, D.C., National Academy Press.

COSEPUP (1983), *Research Briefings*, prepared for the Office of Science and Technology Policy, the National Science Foundation, and selected federal departments and agencies by the Committee on Science, Engineering and Public Policy, Washington, D.C., National Academy Press.

COSPUP (1965), *Basic Research and National Goals*, a report to the Committee on Science and Astronautics, US House of Representatives, by the National Academy of Sciences, Committee on Science and Public Policy, Washington, D.C., US Government Printing Office.

COSPUP (1967), *Applied Science and Technological Progress*, a report to the Committee on Science and Astronautics, US House of Representatives, by the National Academy of Sciences, Committee on Science and Public Policy, Washington, D.C., US Government Printing Office.

CRP (1983), 'Literature models of science for research planning', mimeo, Philadelphia, Center for Research Planning.

DoE (1981), *Federal Energy R & D Priorities*, a report of the Energy Research Advisory Board, Washington, D.C., US Department of Energy.

Field, G. B. (1982), *Astronomy and Astrophysics for the 1980s*, report by the Field Committee to the National Academy of Sciences, Washington, D.C., National Academy Press.

GAO (1981), *Major Science and Technology Issues* (General Accounting Office PAD–81–35), Washington, D.C., GAO.

Greenstein, J. L. (1972), *Astronomy and Astrophysics for the 1970s*, report by the Greenstein Committee to the National Academy of Sciences, Washington, D.C., National Academy of Sciences.

Handler, P. (1970), *Report on the Life Sciences*, report by the Handler

Committee to the National Academy of Sciences, Washington, D.C., National Academy of Sciences.

IIT Research Institute (1968), *Technology in Retrospect and Critical Events in Science*, Washington, D.C., National Science Foundation.

Keyworth, G. A. (1984), 'Four years of Reagan science policy: notable shifts in priorities', *Science* 224, 6 April, pp. 9–13.

Kofmehl, K. (1966), 'COSPUP, Congress and scientific advice', *The Journal of Politics* 28, pp. 100–20.

Little, Arthur D. (1977), *Industrial Perceptions of Technology Opportunities and Relevant Basic Research*, a report submitted to the National Science Foundation by Arthur D. Little Inc., Cambridge, Mass.

Lowrance, W. W. (1977), 'The NAS surveys of fundamental research 1962–1974 in retrospect', *Science* 197, 23 September, pp. 1254–60.

Martin, B. R. and Irvine, J. (1983), 'Assessing basic research: some partial indicators of scientific progress in radio astronomy', *Research Policy* 12 (1983), pp. 61–90.

Mombers, C., Van Heeringen, A., Van Venetie, R. and le Pair, C. (1984), 'Displaying strengths and weaknesses in national R & D performance through document co-citation', Advisory Council for Science Policy, RAWB, 's-Gravenhage (mimeo, FOM–58612).

Narin, F. (1983), 'New approaches to corporate technological intelligence: patent citation network', mimeo, Cherry Hill, N.J., CHI Research.

Narin, F., Carpenter, M. P., and Woolf, P. (1983), 'Technological performance assessments based on patents and patent citations', to be published in *IEEE Transactions on Engineering Management*, mimeo, Cherry Hill, N.J., CHI Research.

NSF (1979), *Unanticipated Benefits from Basic Research*, Washington, D.C., National Science Foundation.

NSF (1980a), *How Basic Research Reaps Unexpected Rewards*, Washington, D.C., National Science Foundation.

NSF (1980b), *The Five-Year Outlook: Problems, Opportunities and Constraints in Science and Technology*, a report by the National Science Foundation, Washington, D.C., US Government Printing Office.

NSF (1981), *Guide to Programs Fiscal Year 1982*, Washington, D.C., National Science Foundation.

NSF (1982a), *National Patterns of Science and Technology Resources 1982*, Washington, D.C., National Science Foundation.

NSF (1982b), *The Five-Year Outlook on Science and Technology 1981*, a report by the National Science Foundation, Washington, D.C., US Government Printing Office.

NSF (1984), *Science Resources Studies Highlights*, 14 May, pp. 1–4, Washington, D.C., National Science Foundation.

Pake, G. E. (1966), *Physics: Survey and Outlook*, report by the Pake Committee to the National Academy of Sciences, Washington, D.C., National Academy of Sciences.

Ronayne, J. (1984), *Science in Government*, London, Edward Arnold.

Rothman, H. (1984), 'Science mapping for strategic planning', in M. Gibbons, P. Gummett, and B. M. Udgaonkar (eds), *Science and Technology Policy in the 1980s and Beyond*, London, Longman.

Shils, E. (ed.) (1968), *Criteria for Scientific Development*, Cambridge, Mass., MIT Press.

Snow, J. A. (1983), 'Research and development: programmes and priorities in a United States mission agency', paper presented at 'Evaluation of R & D Programme Seminar', Commission of the European Communities, Brussels, Belgium, 17–18 October.

Staats, E. B. (1980), 'Statement of Elmer B. Staats, Comptroller General of the United States, before the Subcommittee on Science, Research and Technology of the House Committee on Science and Technology, on long-term planning for national science policy', mimeo, Washington, D.C., General Accounting Office.

TAA (1977), *An Assessment of the Linkage of Research in Electrochemistry with its Ramifications for Industry*, a report submitted to the National Science Foundation by Technical Audit Associates, New York, TAA.

Thimann, K. V. (1966), *The Plant Sciences: Now and in the Coming Decade*, report by the Thimann Committee to the National Academy of Sciences, Washington, D.C., National Academy of Sciences.

US Congress (1976), *National Science and Technology Policy, Organization and Priorities Act of 1976*, Public Law 94–282, 94th Congress, H.R. 10230, 11 May, Washington, D.C., US Government Printing Office.

US House of Representatives, Committee on Science and Technology (1979), *Analysis and Commentary on the First Annual Science and Technology Report*, Washington, D.C., US Government Printing Office.

Walsh, J. (1973), 'Technological innovation: new study sponsored by NSF takes socioeconomic, managerial factors into account', *Science* 180, 25 May, pp. 846–7.

Weinberg, A. M. (1963), 'Criteria for scientific choice', *Minerva* 1, Winter, pp. 159–71.

Westheimer, F. H. (1965), *Chemistry: Opportunities and Needs*, report by the Westheimer Committee to the National Academy of Sciences, Washington, D.C., National Academy of Sciences.

Whitford, A. E. (1964), *Ground-Based Astronomy: A Ten-Year Program*, report by the Whitford Committee to the National Academy of Sciences, Washington, D. C., National Academy of Sciences.

6 Research forecasting in Japan

6.1 Introduction

Japanese state funding for the spectrum of research from basic to applied comes from three principal sources. The Ministry of Education, Science and Culture (Monbusho) is responsible for the support of fundamental research, mainly in the national universities. The Ministry of International Trade and Industry (MITI) is concerned primarily with medium and longer-term R & D programmes that individual firms cannot undertake alone, and which require collective research together with some sharing by the state of the financial and technical risks involved. Finally, the Science and Technology Agency (STA) has the task of financing strategic research lying between the two ends of the pure-applied spectrum, supporting a large proportion of government research institutes. The STA is also charged with overall co-ordination of research between the different ministries,[1] and undertaking infrastructural tasks such as maintaining a statistical data base on Japanese R & D activities. In this section, we consider the main forecasting activities carried out by (i) these three government organisations, (ii) a number of Japan's foremost high-technology companies, and (iii) the country's main technical consultancy organisations.

6.2 Forecasting of fundamental research: Monbusho

The Ministry of Education, Science and Culture (Monbusho) employs three main mechanisms for the support of fundamental research: (i) general funds in the form of block-grants to universities (allocated on a per capita basis); (ii) special funds for the purchase and maintenance of equipment; and (iii) a system of peer-reviewed grants for research projects (which account for less than 5 per cent of the Monbusho budget). In addition, a few research areas have been identified where centralised expermental facilities are essential (such as space science, energy research, and oceanography) and special promotional measures are therefore required to co-ordinate the activities of different research groups.[2]

Monbusho officials interviewed by us were keen to stress that until now the Ministry has respected fully the tradition of academic freedom. Overall policy is set by a Science Council, members (mainly academic scientists) being appointed by the Minister for Education. In addition, a small number of Science Advisers are employed in a consultative role. Because a very high proportion of funds is allocated in the form of per capita research support, there has been little incentive to identify and set future priorities[3] or to redirect resources from one research area to another. Consequently, Monbusho has not developed an interest in longer-term forecasting (which many university scientists would probably oppose anyway), and has not, for example, played any formal role in the STA forecasts described below (although many individual academics have been centrally involved).

The traditional approach of Monbusho to research policy is, however, now being widely questioned. Over the last five years, it has become apparent that in terms of the general level of its technological capability Japan has caught up with the most advanced nations (cf. Moritani, 1983). Since it is now right at the forefront in many areas, the country will have to embark on a policy of indigenous radical innovation, and this will require a much better infrastructural base—in particular, universities able to undertake pioneering fundamental research and provide a flow of suitably trained and creative scientists into industry. Hence, the basic-research system has suddenly become the focus of attention, whereas in the past it contributed only marginally to the technological activities of industry (most basic research and radical technology being imported).

One of the problems identified by the industrialists interviewed was the uneven quality of research in Japanese universities. Only about a dozen universities (the seven former Imperial National Universities, two or three Institutes of Technology and a similar number of private universities) are generally regarded as carrying out front-line research. The rest, at least until very recently, functioned primarily as providers of education rather than performers of research. Another problem is that the links between most universities and industry have traditionally been rather weak. Many professors (especially at national universities) are not used to collaborating with firms, a tendency reinforced by the suspicion and even hostility that certain sectors of the academic community harbour towards industry. A third problem identified was the rapidly escalating cost of research equipment, especially in fields like electronics. Consequently, many universities cannot afford the specialised equipment routinely available in industrial research laboratories that is essential if they are to contribute to the advance of strategically important research fields. For all these reasons, the Japanese university system as currently constituted is not particularly strongly placed to develop the fundamental and strategic science now required to meet national needs. And while these endemic problems in the system could previously be ignored, they have now become a matter of growing concern.

University scientists are consequently being urged to pay more attention to industrial and technological issues, while the system of university tenure and research support is coming under attack for permitting low quality science to flourish and for obstructing attempts to restructure research activity. Similarly, pressures are being exerted on Monbusho to exercise greater influence in selecting areas of research likely to be of strategic importance and to give them financial priority.

In response, the Ministry has recently begun to carry out surveys of individual research fields (for example, electronics, biotechnology and economics). It has also provided funds for research programmes aimed at promoting co-operation between universities, research institutes and industry.[4] However, prospective studies of the likely future impact of different areas of fundamental research have yet to become accepted by Monbusho as part of its overall function.

6.3 Forecasting of strategic research and basic technology: the STA

The Science and Technology Agency was established in 1956 to co-ordinate the research activities of all government ministries and agencies (with the exception of universities and agencies in the humanities). Over time, however, it has also assumed growing responsibility for funding research—largely through a network of institutes —with the result that the Agency accounted in 1981 for 26 per cent of the state budget for science and technology (the corresponding figures for Monbusho and MITI were 49 per cent[5] and 13 per cent respectively—see STA, 1982b, p. 201).

6.3.1 The STA thirty-year forecasts

STA has been involved in two innovative developments of particular interest to this study. The first concerns its work on longer-term forecasting. In 1969, the Agency embarked on what was to prove the first in a series of five-yearly science and technology forecasts. The rationale for undertaking such an exercise—and it still holds true today with equal, if not greater, force—was summarised as follows:

The present age is often referred to as the age of science and technology. Science and technology are indeed the prime movers of our socioeconomic development now, and it would be no exaggeration to say that they will bring about all the major future growth and advances of the nation. In view of this growing importance of science and technology, it is essential to formulate a long-range plan to steadily follow a science and technology policy with definite objectives and with due consideration for its relation to other policies so that science and technology can make efficient advances . . . In framing such a long-range plan, it is most important to foresee likely future socioeconomic changes and to pinpoint those branches of science and technology which will meet renewed requirements. This is especially true of an age in which people's concept of values is rapidly changing and their needs are constantly diversifying and growing in complexity. We have conducted technological forecasting in order to probe into future social and economic needs, to identify those branches of science and technology which will meet such needs, and to explore their technological potentialities. This technological forecast, we hope, will serve as the information on which to base the long-range science and technology plan mentioned earlier and will also be of much help in framing national policies in other fields and in forming research and development plans in private enterprises. [STA, 1972, p. 7.]

The approach adopted by STA was based on four principles. First, the forecast must consider future economic and social needs as well as research and technological developments. Secondly, it must cover holistically *all* areas of science and technology with the potential to meet such needs, rather than focusing on selected individual fields. Thirdly, significant emphasis must be placed on evaluating the relative importance of different research and development tasks and on establishing priorities. Finally, the forecast of a specific scientific or technological development must be seen as having two aspects—an exploratory or predictive element relating to individuals' expectations of change given their accumulated knowledge and experience, and a normative element which involves setting an objective and time-scale within which it is to be achieved. In preparing for the first study, STA began by collecting background information on state-of-the-art techniques available for scientific and technological forecasting—for example, holding seminars to which international authorities on the subject were invited. A General Study Group (consisting of professional forecasters, university researchers, industrialists, R & D managers and scientific journalists) was then set up and entrusted with organising the exercise. Having determined that the forecast should focus on the next thirty years (that is, up to AD 2000), the Study Group divided the fields of science and technology to be covered into five broad areas. Responsibility for these was assigned to five Sectional Groups, each with about seven members. It was also decided that a three-stage Delphi approach should be employed, with the results of each round of the survey constituting the basis for the subsequent questionnaire.

The next step was to choose a sufficiently large and representative sample of experts. It was estimated that 4,000 would be needed to cover all fields adequately. Most importantly, it was decided to include experts with cultural as well as scientific backgrounds, and to ensure that a significant proportion (nearly 40 per cent of those eventually chosen) should have a sufficiently broad knowledge to pass judgement on several scientific or technological fields. The three principal sectors of academia, government and industry all had to be thoroughly covered, while efforts were also made to ensure that younger researchers were well represented. The experts were selected from a list of individuals recommended by government agencies and academic societies, from those who had recently written on technological forecasting or future-orientated issues, and from people working in industry or research institutes with particular specialised knowledge.

The purpose of the first questionnaire, which was sent out in September 1970 to 1,500 of the experts, was to establish what were likely to be the main social and economic 'needs' over the following ten years, and the next ten to thirty years, together with any developments in research that were felt necessary for these needs to be met. The Sectional Groups—which had prepared a list of some 500 questions to help the experts in this task—subsequently analysed the responses, and identified around 650 important research developments. The second questionnaire, which was sent to all 4,000 experts four months later, asked them to assess the relative importance of each potential development, estimate when it was likely to be realised, and make a judgement (on a three-point scale) about their own competence to pronounce on the subject. These questions were repeated in the third questionnaire, which also contained the results of the previous round. The experts thus had a chance to re-assess their judgements in the light of the majority views; where they still disagreed significantly with the latter, they were asked to give reasons. In addition, respondents were invited to propose appropriate government measures (for example, a funding initiative, training programme or R & D co-ordination scheme) to expedite each research development. Finally, the questionnaires were analysed, and the results summarised in a widely circulated STA report (STA, 1972). Table 6.1, which lists some of the predicted developments in the area of information technology, provides an illustration of the type of findings that emerged.

That the STA forecast was taken seriously by those participating is evident from the high survey response-rate achieved, which averaged between 76 and 80 per cent for the three questionnaires. As for the utility of the forecasts, this will be discussed below, but its impact was sufficiently great for the exercise to be repeated in 1974/75 (STA, 1976) and again in 1981/82 (STA, 1982a). A very similar approach was adopted in both these later forecasts, the main difference being that a two-stage procedure was employed, with members of the Sectional Groups being used to identify the technological developments to be listed in the first questionnaire rather than a preliminary set of questions being sent out to experts. Another, less important difference was that the number of experts surveyed was reduced to just over 2,000, while still ensuring that industry, government organisations, and universities and research institutes were approximately equally represented.

Most of those interviewed in our study judged the STA forecasts to have been reasonably successful, citing the following benefits. First, they provide a mechanism to ensure that researchers in all sectors, along with policy-makers in government and industry, are periodically forced to think systematically about the longer-term future. In the absence of such forecasts, more immediate problems tend to crowd out attempts to face up to the more distant future. In short, the STA exercises lead to clear strategic benefits.

Secondly, the forecasts yield a general summary of what is happening, or likely to happen, across the entire range of R & D activities. They therefore permit more 'holistic' vision-making, enabling the potential longer-term cross-impacts of developments in one research field on another to be identified at an early stage. The Japanese were, for example, among the first to appreciate the significance of 'mechatronics' (the incorporation of electronics in machines) and the impending importance of multidiscipline-based information technology (as indicated in Table 6.1), and hence to be in a position to derive many of the subsequent dramatic benefits.

A third advantage of the STA approach to forecasting is that, by surveying comprehensively the intentions and visions (and thus indirectly the current strategic R & D activity) of the industrial research community, it provides a useful mechanism for synthesising major research trends across science-based sectors. The survey results thus enable firms to see in a general way what their competitors believe are the most important technological developments to be made in a particular sector and when they are likely to be achieved. If necessary, they can then adjust their own R & D strategies accordingly. It is the existence of such surveys that is in part responsible for the strong agreement among Japanese firms as to what are likely to be the critical future developments in their sector. In particular, the STA surveys were reported by industrialists as providing a general framework for the more detailed sector forecasts routinely carried out by industrial associations, which play a central role in creating this consensus. Most importantly, despite taking a longer-term perspective, the STA forecasts have by all accounts proved remarkably accurate.[6]

Lastly, the STA forecasts provide a useful mechanism for helping government establish national priorities in allocating resources. Requirements for infrastructural support can be identified from the 'bottom-up' by industry, rather than being imposed in a 'top-down' process by state-planners who may not always be in touch with industrial problems. Although such forecasts do not, in themselves, lead directly to policy decisions, the systematic information which they generate helps narrow down the range of different views that can be held on a particular R & D-related issue, bringing eventual consensus that much closer. Hence, while it is difficult to point out specific direct consequences of the STA surveys, they have clearly had a diffuse effect on R & D planning—for example, helping the STA ensure that the activities of its own laboratories are kept broadly in line with changing longer-term R & D needs.

Besides the various benefits associated with the STA forecasts, it is also necessary to note certain drawbacks which have only come to the fore over the last few years. In particular, the STA forecasts, in common with all studies based upon Delphi techniques, have an inherent tendency towards conservatism (see note 6). The fact that the forecasts have failed to anticipate some of the more creative scientific advances mattered little when the country could rely on importing basic technology developed on the basis of the research efforts of other nations. Now, as Japan is forced to rely increasingly on the fruits of its own research endeavours, this problem is, in the opinion of those interviewed by us, becoming more acute.

A second and related disadvantage associated with STA-type forecasts is that, precisely because they do create consensus on research priorities, there is a resulting uniformity in the technologies developed which can breed excessive competition between firms within certain industrial sectors (the chemical sector was cited as an example). Clearly, methods for resisting these tendencies towards

Table 6.1   Illustrative results from the 1972 STA forecast

Information Technology

Subject
42. Commercialisation of letter readers which can read clearly hand-written manuscripts containing Chinese hieroglyphic characters and the two Japanese alphabets. (These machines will have a reading error ratio of less than 1% and will be able to read 'educational' Chinese characters which are of the standard lettering style and have about 15 strokes per character.)
43. Commercialisation of voice input equipment which can accommodate input data containing not only numerals but also several hundred Japanese words. (These machines will be put into use only with specially trained persons who speak with clear and correct pronunciation.)
44. Development of pattern recognition techniques which can recognise artificial, complicated patterns (e.g. any kind of drawings) at a speed comparable to that of humans.
45. Development of pattern recognition techniques which can recognise natural patterns (natural figures such as human faces) at a speed comparable to that of humans.
46. Development of pattern recognition techniques which can identify individuals by means of voice patterns ('voice prints').
47. Development of techniques for detecting smells and tastes (kinds, qualities, etc.).
48. Techniques for translating foreign documents (in English) into Japanese.
49. Development of automatic simultaneous-translation machines which can handle standard business conversations (Japanese-English).
50. Development of techniques for high-density data storage at the molecular level (functioning like DNA and RNA).
51. Development of highly durable memory elements which can withstand magnetic interference, electrical trouble and fire and are not subject to accidental erasure of information.
52. Commercialisation of highly sensitive (sensitivity equal or superior to that of films) optical memory elements which are freely erasable and re-useable.
53. Commercialisation of large-capacity and cheap (similar to magnetic tapes and discs) data films requiring no mechanical access and allowing access at a higher speed than those requiring mechanical access.
54. Commercialisation of light memory utilizing laser holography to greatly increase the memory capacity required for information retrieval.

Source: STA (1972, pp. 84–5).

Poll No.	Respondents	Importance (%) h	m	l	Realisable (%)	Unrealisable (%)	Time of realisation	Reason for non-realisation (%)	Govt. measure (%)
2	431	60	35	5	91	9		A 5 B 0 C 2 D 2	A 38 B 16 C 20 D 2 E 28
3	329	82	16	2	97	3			
2	426	56	28	6	93	7		A 6 B 0 C 1 D 1	A 39 B 17 C 17 D 2 E 30
3	328	76	20	4	99	1			
2	423	63	34	3	85	15		A 12 B 0 C 1 D 2	A 35 B 19 C 22 D 3 E 28
3	323	81	18	1	94	6			
2	420	51	46	3	85	15		A 11 B 0 C 1 D 1	A 30 B 20 C 19 D 3 E 32
3	319	62	35	3	90	10			
2	414	39	52	9	92	8		A 7 B 0 C 0 D 1	A 34 B 16 C 16 D 3 E 33
3	323	30	65	5	96	4			
2	386	21	44	35	73	27		A 23 B 0 C 0 D 4	A 16 B 21 C 16 D 10 E 39
3	305	11	55	34	71	29			
2	423	58	37	5	91	9		A 8 B 0 C 2 D 0	A 35 B 16 C 20 D 2 E 32
3	319	80	18	2	96	4			
2	413	51	42	7	67	33		A 27 B 0 C 2 D 4	A 27 B 19 C 21 D 4 E 33
3	312	66	29	5	72	28			
2	365	52	38	10	71	29		A 24 B 0 C 0 D 5	A 20 B 25 C 20 D 6 E 33
3	283	70	27	3	68	32			
2	390	52	35	13	72	28		A 21 B 0 C 6 D 2	A 25 B 14 C 21 D 6 E 36
3	296	76	19	5	80	20			
2	406	51	45	4	94	6		A 5 B 0 C 1 D 0	A 35 B 14 C 17 D 2 E 35
3	290	66	30	4	98	2			
2	399	67	30	3	96	4		A 4 B 0 C 0 D 0	A 43 B 11 C 17 D 1 E 32
3	318	88	11	1	99	1			
2	386	49	46	5	97	3		A 2 B 0 C 1 D 0	A 41 B 9 C 15 D 1 E 35
3	303	59	38	3	99	1			

conservatism and competition on the basis of too narrow a range of technology have to be devised for future STA forecasts if the technological competitiveness of Japanese industry is to be preserved into the 1980s.

6.3.2 *The STA ERATO programme*

The second STA initiative we shall consider is the 'Programme for Exploratory Research for Advanced Technology' (ERATO). This was launched in 1981 (under the control of the Research Development Corporation of Japan) with the aim of supporting the basic research needed to establish creative new indigenous technology, and reflected the realisation, noted earlier, that Japan had to promote more research of a fundamental nature if it was to create the innovative 'seeds' for the science-based industries of tomorrow.[7]

Beginning with seed-money of 600 million yen (about $2.5 million) in 1981, the programme has grown rapidly, and is scheduled to have a budget of 8 billion yen (some $40 million) in 1987. The overall structure of ERATO is shown in Figure 6.1, with details of five of the six main research themes approved by 1983 given in Table 6.2. The Agency describes this programme as an

innovative flexible research system where researchers from private enterprises, universities, and public research laboratories, including some from overseas, are gathered together under outstanding project leaders. [STA, 1982b, p. 50.]

[The] fields of research are broad and centred around a basic understanding of the natures of materials and life. The fields are outside the traditional academic disciplines and it is hoped that the program will generate breakthroughs in various interdisciplinary fields. It is also hoped that they will bridge the gap between science and technology. [STA, 1983a, p. 23.]

In selecting the programme research areas, STA drew upon a variety of inputs—including consultations with industry and various forecasts, in particular their own recent study. Also important were the extensive discussions leading up to a parallel MITI 'Research and Development Project of Basic Technology for Future Industries' (which is considered in section 6.4). These discussions revealed the need for a new initiative on fundamental materials research. This would not only have long-term applications across numerous emerging technologies, but would link in well with the MITI programme. Furthermore, STA saw ERATO as a means of developing better links between universities, research institutes and industry, on research with intrinsic intellectual interest as well as strategic significance.[8] However, this has inevitably created some friction with Monbusho which feels, on the one hand, that the programme should

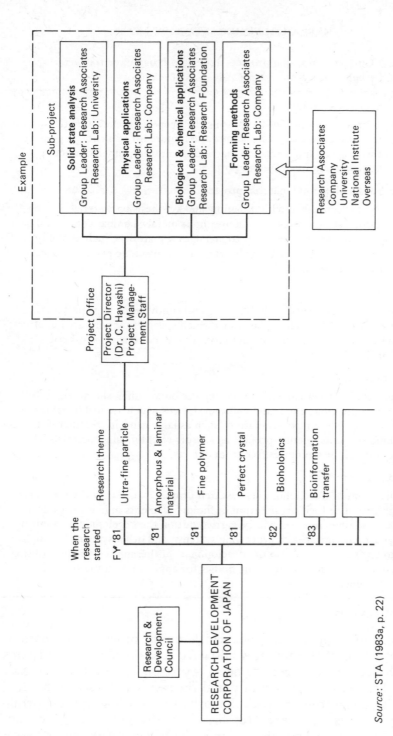

Source: STA (1983a, p. 22)

Figure 6.1 Organisation of Exploratory Research for Advanced Technology

Table 6.2   Outline of research projects under the Programme for Exploratory Research for Advanced Technology

---

1. Ultra-fine particle project

   This project is concerned with exploring the properties characteristic of ultra-fine particles (whose size is about one-hundredth of a cholera germ) to extend the range of application to magnetic memories, superconducting materials, separation of viruses and others.

2. Amorphous and laminar material project

   This project is concerned with designing and synthesising materials having special atomic structures (such as amorphous metals, laminar compounds, and non-equilibrium compounds) to create new materials, such as highly corrosion-resistant materials, highly transparent magnetic materials, special composite materials and others.

3. Fine polymer project

   This project is concerned with designing and synthesising large polymers of high added value, such as plastics to which special functions are imparted (e.g. biocompatibility, semiconductivity, superconductivity, synthetic functional film, etc.).

4. Perfect crystal project

   This project is concerned with extracting the outstanding characteristics of electrostatic induction semiconductor devices which are highly valued as promising ICs in the next generation (such as large capacity rectifier elements, switching elements, picture-processing sensors etc.) by using materials with perfect crystalline structures free from defects.

5. Bioholonics project

   The main aim of this bioholonics research project is to clarify the mechanism of aggregation and self-organisation of 'holon' elements in living organisms. At the same time, research will be carried out on the development of molecular machines, image-data processing systems, and other systems for application to engineering, and also the development of therapy techniques utilising the self-control functions of living bodies for application in the field of medical science.

Source: STA (1983a, p. 22).

have been its responsibility, but which, on the other, finds it hard to counter STA criticism that it would have been unable to identify this research need or to target the necessary resources. Rather than wait for the basic-science community and the associated research-funding agency to come to terms with the task of identifying and supporting promising areas of science (as has been the policy—not wholly successful—in the US), the Japanese have taken early and decisive action. While there are certainly associated dangers in such action, the policy has been informed by detailed background information and extensive consultation. Thus far, it appears to be proving a success.

6.4 Forecasting of basic technology: MITI

Responsibility for research and development nearer to the stage of industrial application has traditionally rested with the Ministry of International Trade and Industry (MITI) and its Agency of Industrial Science and Technology (AIST). MITI describes its role in the following terms:

The Ministry of International Trade and Industry has always aggressively promoted industrial technological policies with the aim of establishing Japan as a 'technology-based nation'. The basic policy of the Ministry is to provide an environment in which the vitality of the private sector, the foundation of national technological development, can be maximised. However, in those areas where a high degree of financial and technical risk is involved and where the private sector alone finds it difficult to smoothly carry out the development programs despite the economic importance and urgency of the programs, the Ministry takes strong steps to promote such programs in organic linkage between industry, universities, and the State. [AIST, 1982a, p. 2.]

In line with these responsibilities, MITI has in recent years reorientated its research policy to support the 'core' or 'basic' technologies identified as likely to have strategic importance over coming decades. The means by which these promising areas are selected draw heavily on foresight activities, so it is worth discussing them in detail. The main R & D programmes currently supported by the AIST include: (a) the 'Sunshine Project' to develop new energy technologies (initiated in 1974); (b) the 'Moonlight Project' to develop energy-conservation technologies (begun in 1978); (c) the 'National Research and Development Program' (or 'Large-Scale Projects') to create major new industrial technologies (for example, high-speed computers); and (d) the 'Research and Development Project of Basic Technologies for New Industries', which is described below.[9]

MITI has an organisational structure based on divisions corresponding to the main industrial sectors. Each division normally operates a long-term plan for its particular industry, which it revises every three to five years. In addition, an attempt is made during the planning period to integrate the various sectoral plans and construct an overall MITI 'vision' of the future for Japanese industry.

Based on this industrial vision, MITI and AIST draw up a long-term R & D plan, which is again revised every three years or so. In this, MITI attempts to pick up early research tendencies, to construct 'visions' of how new technologies are likely to develop, to formulate an appropriate overall R & D policy, to select priority research fields and to initiate special projects within them. However, it is crucially important to stress one point that is frequently overlooked by foreign commentators. The process involved here is *not* one of centralised 'top-down' planning by MITI, which then imposes its objectives on industry and others. Instead, most influence tends to flow in precisely the opposite direction, with MITI's role largely confined to 'tapping into' the views of firms and establishing where the consensus lies. Only as a last resort are priorities imposed—for example, to give one industrial sector's agreed programme precedence over another's. In order to see how this process works, let us examine how the MITI programme on 'Basic Technology for Future (or Next-Generation) Industries' (details of which are given in Table 6.3) was constructed.[10]

Formally, if not in practice, the programme on 'Basic Technology for Future Industries' emerged from two main sources: *The Vision of MITI Policies in the 1980s* (MITI, 1980a and 1980b); and *Toward New Research and Development* (AIST, 1981a). The former, hereafter referred to as the *1980s' Vision*, was a report produced by MITI's Industrial Structure Council, a body consisting of industrialists, academics, consumers and trade unionists.[11] The Council had compiled similar long-term industrial visions in 1963 and 1971, the latter having been particularly influential in highlighting the need for Japan to shift to more knowledge-intensive industries.[12]

The *1980s' Vision* took as its starting point the fact that the Japanese economy has finally achieved the national goal of the previous hundred years—that of reaching the level of Western industrial nations. It was therefore necessary, the report argued, to establish new long-term national goals and to begin planning a strategy for their realisation. Three goals were proposed: (a) to contribute more positively to the international community (for example, through promoting free trade, carrying out more of the world's research and helping developing countries); (b) to strive to overcome the limitations imposed by the country's shortage of natural resources and energy; and (c) to try to harmonise continued economic dynamism with an improved quality of life (cf. MITI, 1980b, p. 4). The role that technology would have to play in achieving such goals was particularly stressed, with a number of research objectives being identified. These included R & D on new energy

Table 6.3   Outline of research projects under the Research and Development
Project of Basic Technology for Future Industries

Project	Outline
New Materials ($5,424,000)	
1. High performance ceramics	○ Development of structural or engineering ceramics which are hard, rust-free, dimensionally accurate, and suitable for high-temperature applications. ○ The ceramics are expected to be applied in such high-tech fields as nuclear power, new energy, and aerospace, as well as in improving the efficiency of energy-saving thermal engines.
2. Synthetic membrane for new separation technology	○ Development of synthetic membranes which by utilising differences in the properties of matter freely separate and refine mixed gases or liquids. ○ The membranes, when developed and applied to separation and refining processes in the chemical industry, will bring about energy-saving and pollution-free factories.
3. Synthetic metals	○ Development of synthetic metals (polymer materials) which, unlike real metals, are light-weight and corrosion resistant, but still electrically conductive. ○ The metals will replace copper and aluminium used in electrical wires and cables, and also are good candidates for superconductive materials.
4. High performance plastics	○ Development of high performance plastics, light but metal-strong polymers, using high crystalisation techniques. ○ The plastics are expected to replace aluminium and steel as structural materials, and are also considered as super-strength materials which are elastic and electrically insulating.
5. Advanced alloys with controlled crystalline structures	○ Development of strong alloys, exceeding the performance of conventional alloys, through single crystalisation and grain-refining techniques. ○ The alloys will improve the reliability of nuclear reactors, aircraft, and aerospace equipment, and also contribute to energy conservation.
6. Advanced composite materials	○ Development of advanced composite materials, lighter than aluminium alloys and stronger than steel, with specified strengths and hardness for highly reliable structural materials.

Table 6.3 (*cont.*)

Project	Outline
6. Advanced composite materials (*cont.*)	○ The composite materials are considered indispensable for further development of machinery such as aircraft, cars, space equipment, and their lightness will also contribute to energy conservation.
[Bio-technology] ($2,700,000)	
1. Bio-reactor	○ Development of bioreactor technology for new chemical reactions that use micro-organisms or enzymes. ○ The technology which involves reactions under normal temperature and pressure is advantageous over conventional chemical reactions, and can realise energy-saving and pollution-free chemical industry.
2. Large-scale cell cultivation	○ Development of a method to replace a serum, such as from the unborn calf, presently supplemented in medium to support proliferation of mammalian cells in culture, for various cell lines and make submerged cultures possible. This is one of the essential basic technologies for the bio-industry. ○ The method for serum-free medium and/or submerged culture will drastically reduce the cost of large-scale cultivation and time for purification of products.
3. Utilisation of recombinant DNA	○ Development of DNA recombinant technology, another basic technology essential to bio-industry, could be used not only to obtain hormones and enzymes, but also to produce bulk commodity chemicals. ○ The technology makes it possible to create new micro-organisms to be used in the production process of chemicals.
[New electronic devices] ($2,692,000)	
1. Super-lattice devices	○ Development of super-lattice devices that have an extremely fine structure tailored to atomic scale, and utilise new electronic effects arising from such a structure. ○ The device is expected to realise ultra-high frequency and ultra-high speed operation at room temperature.

2. Three-dimensional ICs	Development of three dimensional ICs by alternatively stacking semiconductor layers for active elements and insulator layers for separation.
	○ The ICs will be ultra-large-scale and have monolithic integration of various functional elements such as for sensors, processors, memories, and displays to realise further miniaturisation of computers.
3. Fortified ICs for extreme conditions	○ Development of fortified ICs that can withstand severe conditions such as high-energy irradiation, high temperatures, mechanical vibrations, and shocks, to construct electronic systems reliably functioning under extreme conditions.
	○ The ICs are expected to expand the usage of computers in various new areas including space development and nuclear power generation.

Source: STA (1982b, Table 8–6 of English translation).

sources and conservation, the development of more knowledge-intensive and innovative technologies, and more basic research on such next-generation technologies as genetic engineering, biotechnology and nuclear fusion (cf. ibid., p. 15).[13]

The formulation of an R & D strategy to achieve the three new national goals set out in the *1980s' Vision* was one of the main themes of the other key document preceding the establishment of the programme on 'Basic Technology for Future Industries'—the report entitled *Toward New Research and Development* (AIST, 1981a). This was produced by the 'Study Meeting for the Formulation of a Long-Term Industrial Technology Development Program', a group of about twenty industrialists, academics, research institute staff and science commentators set up by AIST in 1977. The study group considered a wide range of evidence including: (a) an opinion survey of experts on the technological level of different industrial sectors in Japan relative to overseas and how this was likely to change over the coming years; (b) a systematic search through the forecasting literature to try to identify the emerging or rapidly expanding industries of the next ten years; and (c) extrapolations into the future of national R & D expenditure to determine whether the continuation of existing trends would be sufficient to reach the targets of 2.5 per cent and 3 per cent of GDP set for 1985 and 1990 respectively. In addition, extensive discussions were held with industrialists and academics concerning R & D priorities. These yielded a total of 365 industrial problems seen as requiring research for their solution, and capable of being overcome by the year 2000.

Like the *1980's Vision, Toward New Research and Development* stressed the importance of basic technology (and hence strategic research), listing four reasons why government support for such work should be increased: (a) because of the high risks involved; (b) because it is potentially applicable to a wide range of industries, i.e. it is 'generic' in nature; (c) because it is subject to increasing international competition; and (d) because it has become increasingly difficult for Japan to rely on overseas sources for basic technology (cf. AIST, 1981a, p. 41). As for predicting *which* basic technologies were likely to prove most significant, the report identified three crucial technological trends—towards miniaturisation, towards the more intensive use of information-processing facilities in products and processes, and towards systems incorporating several different technologies (for example, electronics and machinery)—which, it argued, pointed to the increasing prominence of micro-technology, information technology, and composite materials technology (ibid., pp. 42–54). More specifically, the report suggested that new materials, biotechnology, and new electronic devices were research fields likely to yield radical innovations forming the basis of the next generation of technologies and industries.

In 1981, even before the final report of the 'Study Meeting for the Formulation of a Long-Term Industrial Technology Development Program' had been formally submitted,[14] the Agency of Industrial Science and Technology decided to embark on the 'Basic Technology for Future Industries' programme. In the MITI document summarising the programme, the need for such an initiative was justified in terms of the fact that Japan still lagged five to ten years behind the United States and Europe in those basic technologies likely to create the new industries of the 1990s (cf. AIST, 1981b, p. 1). The three fields chosen for support were precisely those highlighted in *Toward New Research and Development*, namely new materials, biotechnology, and new electronic devices. Within these, twelve specific research areas were chosen, according to the following selection criteria:

(a) highly innovative technologies, the development of which is likely to have far-reaching effects;
(b) technologies where R & D will take roughly ten years and require huge investments, rendering projects too risky for private firms to attempt alone;
(c) technologies already being developed by other advanced countries and which therefore require rapid implementation of research (cf. AIST, 1982b, p. 6).

As noted earlier, many foreign commentators fall victim to the illusion of 'Japan Incorporated', in which social, economic and industrial priorities are seen as being determined centrally and then accepted by an unquestioning public and industry. (While Japanese industrial policy may have been directed largely by MITI in the two post-war decades, this no longer applies to the same extent.) In analysing the origins of the 'Basic Technology for Future Industries' programme, it is tempting to ascribe the major role to a small heroic band of MITI officials who produced the early draft of the *1980s' Vision*, who serviced the 'Study Meeting for the Formulation of a Long-Term Industrial Technology Development Program', and who drew up the detailed plan for the resultant research programme. However, that would be to completely misrepresent the situation.[15]

While formally it may appear that strategic research priorities are determined by the interplay between MITI-co-ordinated activities (such as the study meeting) and industry, in practice they are usually 'prepared' beforehand by informal working groups attached to the main industrial trade associations (the members of which include all major companies with an interest in the sector concerned). The companies are quick to become aware when a new government initiative is in the offing, and collectively hammer out in the relevant informal working group their common longer-term priorities, using, for example, forecasts commissioned by industrial associations from consultancy organisations such as the Nomura and Mitsubishi Research Institutes (see section 6.6). The working groups thus ensure that the views put forward to MITI represent the consensus among the leading firms in each industrial sector on the long-term basic technologies in which they wish to become involved. MITI's role, therefore, is confined to the following: (a) providing an overall framework in which consensus on long-term industrial and research priorities can emerge (for example, by ensuring that accurate up-to-date R & D statistics are freely available); (b) acting as a catalyst in the generation of consensus (for example, through discussions with industrialists and researchers, and through periodically pub-lishing long-term 'visions' to foster debate); (c) monitoring con-tinuously the views of firms and industrial associations to see when consensus appears to emerge on a particular issue, publicising the results within the relevant industrial sectors, and hence providing feedback into the consensus-generating process; and (d) within the limits of overall budgetary constraints, attempting to obtain agreement among the different industrial sectors as to priorities. In short, Japanese long-term R & D priorities on applied and strategic research emerge in a 'bottom-up process' rather than being decided centrally by MITI officials. As we argue in the next chapter, this is a process from which other countries have much to learn.

6.5 Forecasting of strategic and applied research: industry

In Japan, approximately 75 per cent of total national expenditure on research and development is borne by private industry, well above the average of about 50 per cent for OECD countries. The fact that the government share has been relatively low in international terms is one reason why the country's research activities have previously tended to be concentrated on applied R & D, with comparatively little effort being devoted to fundamental, or even strategic research, at least until recently. The five years up to 1983, however, witnessed a rapid increase in R & D expenditure by firms (from about 2 per cent to 2.5 per cent of sales),[16] with much more going into longer-term R & D to develop new 'generic' technologies (i.e. technologies likely to be incorporated in a wide range of products or processes).

Firms have at the same time been exerting increasing pressure on MITI to redirect its R & D support for industry towards more basic research. One reason for this is the realisation (mentioned earlier) that in many industrial sectors Japanese companies are now at the forefront and can no longer rely on a strategy of importing basic technology. Another is the fact that certain countries and foreign firms are beginning to take steps to ensure that the previous 'leakage' of promising developments is curbed. A third factor, however, has been the growing recognition of the crucial role that the state can play in providing a framework within which firms in a particular sector can join together to develop collaborative programmes for tackling the risky longer-term research needed to develop new generic technologies.

In high-technology sectors, most Japanese firms participate actively in the relevant industrial associations. These undertake a considerable amount of longer-term forecasting, much of which is commissioned from consultancy organisations (see section 6.6)— the results being used both by firms and MITI. Recent forecasts have highlighted the need to upgrade the general quality of university research in order to ensure appropriately qualified graduates are available to staff emerging new areas of industrial R & D. As was noted in section 6.2, some restructuring of the support mechanisms for university research is thus seen by firms to be necessary if that research training is to become more relevant to industrial needs.

Among the organisations visited in Japan was the Long-Term

Credit Bank (LTCB). The time-horizon for investments made by the LTCB is generally seven to ten years. It has therefore undertaken a considerable amount of medium- and long-term forecasting (of technological as well as market trends), both for deciding its own investment strategy and for providing consultancy advice to individual firms. The forecasts suggest that the next ten to twenty years will witness a fundamental structural change in Japanese industry. Basic industries such as iron and steel, chemicals, aluminium refining and ship-building, will account for a declining proportion of total industrial output, while the share of high-technology industries seems set to rise from 2 per cent in 1980 to between 15 and 20 per cent by the mid-1990s (cf. LTCB, 1983a, p. i). The LTCB has consequently set up a special group to analyse likely technological developments in such leading sectors as robotics, office automation, new materials, biotechnology, computers and opto-electronics (ibid.). In addition, quantitative forecasts have been compiled for the projected sales and rates of growth in these sectors, the figures being based on individual studies undertaken by industrial associations and on the consensus views of firms as to likely trends (see, for example, LTCB, 1983b).

Of the five industrial firms visited in Japan, three were in the electrical and electronics sector[17] and two in the chemicals sector. Let us first consider the former.

As in most Japanese companies, the percentage of turnover devoted to R & D has been increasing in Company H (a major electronics firm); it stood at 5.6 per cent in 1984 and is scheduled to reach 7 per cent in the near future, with over a quarter being devoted to longer-term, high-risk research (such as in new materials or biochips). Monitoring of technical trends and identification of important new research areas are regarded as increasingly vital tasks by the company,[18] the view being that the electronics industry is on the threshold of a qualitative technological transformation. The company has a large 'advanced technology department' of some fifty staff. Of these, ten are employed scanning newspapers, magazines, research journals, conference proceedings, and forecasting reports from such organisations as Battelle, SRI International and the Mitsubishi Research Institute; others operate the corporate 'technology information centre' which has routine access to a large number of data bases in Japan and overseas. In addition, another sixty staff work in a patent-survey office, monitoring and analysing patenting activity, while twenty eminent university professors (including two in the US) are retained as consultants to feed the latest scientific information into the corporate planning and R & D functions. Besides these extensive monitoring activities, the company also engages in a considerable amount of long-term forecasting (generally with a time-horizon of between ten and fifteen years). It regularly commissions consultancy organisations to prepare technological and market forecasts in very specific areas, as well as subscribing to multi-client studies for broader perspectives.

Armed with this wealth of information, the members of the Corporate Engineering Committee of Company H are in a good position to identify potentially important new technologies at an early stage. The company then mounts what is known as an 'urgent project'. There were in 1983 about thirty such projects (one, for example, was on domestic solar technology), each led by a senior researcher reporting directly to the head of corporate R & D and able to recruit freely from any of the firm's laboratories. The task of the project teams is not only to attempt to develop new basic technology, but also to maintain close links with research groups in universities and elsewhere so that the company can move quickly to take advantage of scientific developments as and when they occur.

Likewise, Company I (one of the world's leading suppliers of communications systems, computers, electronic devices and consumer electronic products) has been placing increasing emphasis on new technology, and currently spends 5.5 per cent of sales on R & D (and a further 5 per cent on production-engineering development), of which about one-fifth is devoted to longer-term research. The company reported growing concern with the need to identify and master new 'core' or 'generic' technologies. In contrast with *single-purpose* technologies, where the risk of failure can be very high, generic technologies (for example, opto-electronics, voice and image-processing and digital technology) are seen as relatively risk-free in that they can be used within many product lines. In identifying emerging new technologies, Company I adopts a similar approach to that of Company H. It undertakes extensive monitoring of R & D in other firms,[19] universities[20] and research institutes. Of particular interest is the fact that the company carries out detailed historical case-studies of the 'seeds' of current generic technologies, hoping that this will give them a better understanding of their likely future development. As for more traditional forecasting, the firm commissions studies from outside consultancy organisations as well as carrying out long-term forecasts in-house. The results of these and the publicly available forecasts (for example, those produced by the STA and industrial associations) are regarded by senior management as providing essential background information in helping them to revise their rolling five-year R & D plan.

In Company J (another large electronics firm), the ratio of R & D expenditure to sales is a little lower but is rising rapidly, having increased from 3.8 per cent in 1980/81 to 4.3 per cent in 1981/82 and 4.8 per cent in 1982/83. Much of this is targeted on strategic areas, especially electronics and energy-related products, and, as with its competitors, the emphasis placed on longer-term strategic research is being significantly increased.[21] Each of the company's six research laboratories has a planning office, and once a year all the planners meet to develop a long-term R & D plan for the next ten years, although this is only fully mapped out for the first five years. Inputs into this planning process include extensive monitoring by the company, commissioned forecasts from Japanese and US consultancy organisations, STA and MITI forecasts, and work by an associated Company J Research Institute. Of this Institute's fifty staff, between ten and fifteen are engaged in forecasting, mainly on behalf of senior management in the parent company, but also for outside organisations on a consultancy basis.

One of the most important studies being carried out at the time of interviewing by the Company J Research Institute was entitled 'Electronics Technology Development Strategy—Towards the 21st Century'. This exercise, which was commissioned by the National Institute for Research Advancement (NIRA), seeks to identify the basic technologies that will be needed to meet specified social and economic needs over the next twenty years. Up to 1983, work had focused on the 'demand' side. The procedure adopted was to set up a research committee of ten experts, mostly industrialists, who, with the aid of results from an extensive literature and patent survey, identified several hundred development-targets to be achieved by the electronics industry over the period up to the end of this century. A structured questionnaire was then sent to 500 researchers at Company J, the results of which were used to evaluate quantitatively possible new basic technologies in terms of (a) their 'application rate'—that is, the percentage of the development-targets identified to which the particular technology could contribute; and (b) their 'competitiveness', an indicator measuring how indispensable each technology is likely to be for achieving the various development-targets. Among the areas identified as in greatest need of more research were electronic devices, opto-electronics, bio-electronics and new materials. The study is significant because it represents one of the first attempts to adopt a quantitative approach to the 'demand' side of technological forecasting. In 1984, the Company J Research Institute embarked on the other part of the study—an attempt to forecast the 'seeds' of new basic technologies.

Again, a quantitative approach is being employed, but this time the questionnaire is also being sent to researchers in other electronics companies.

It was at the time of writing too soon to estimate the success of this study[22] since the final report had not yet been produced, but a similar exercise in the early 1970s was apparently found most useful by the electronics industry. That study looked at future technological trends, the impact they were likely to have on industry, and the probable time-scales involved. In Japan, such sector-wide forecasts provide an essential link between the macro-forecasts by the STA and MITI, and firms' internal forecasts (often restricted to a relatively narrow range of products). From the point of view of industry, the sector forecasts, because they are more specific than the macro-forecasts, are much more valuable for planning corporate R & D strategy. Equally, the sector studies, based as they are on a synthesis of industrial views, constitute a key input into discussions within MITI and the STA. The situation is well summed up in the following statements made by two senior managers interviewed at Japanese electronics firms:

In Japan, industry gets together in industrial associations. These carry out collective forecasts and decide what risky new basic research needs to be done. We then go to the government and ask them for help to do the work. The results will subsequently be made public and all firms can then utilise them . . . So in the development of new MITI programmes, a great deal is first decided by industrial associations. These then give their proposals to MITI. All MITI themes are decided by consensus among firms. The role of MITI is just to coordinate and synthesise. [Interview, 1983.]

There are about 600 industrial associations altogether, although only two dozen are really active. We are a member of twelve. The Japanese Association for Electronic Industries Promotion is always doing studies of the future. Industry gets together, arrives at a consensus (sometimes with MITI people there), and then puts this to MITI. MITI is very good at pinpointing and taking up consensus items and giving support. [Interview, 1983.]

Finally, let us consider the forecasting activities of the two chemical companies visited in Japan. In the case of Company K (a large chemical firm which has diversified into pharmaceuticals, medical care, foodstuffs, and, more recently, biotechnology, new materials, and alternative sources of energy), research is undertaken mainly in a central laboratory and various divisional laboratories, but also in the associated Company K Institute of Life Sciences, and, since 1982, in an associated biotechnology research institute. Whereas the company was originally based around heavy chemicals, a third of its R & D budget is now devoted to the life sciences and biotechnology.[23]

Like all the Japanese firms visited, Company K places great emphasis on monitoring research developments, in particular through commissioned work at universities in order to foster contact between its own staff and academic researchers. It also engages in systematic foresight activities, making use of the three main types of forecast: those by MITI and the STA; multi-client forecasts by Japanese and US consultancy organisations of selected technologies or industrial sectors; and studies specially commissioned by the company targeted towards more specific technological areas. While the general government forecasts, and even the sector forecasts, may contain little of which the company is not already aware (they are, after all, no more than a synthesis of its own views and those of other firms in the industry), they are nevertheless seen as useful in persuading senior management of the potential importance of new research areas. As a result, forecasting of research trends contributes vital inputs to the company's five- and ten-year plans.

The situation at Company L is very similar. Originally just a manufacturer of synthetic fibres, the firm has over the last decade been diversifying rapidly into new areas of advanced technology such as biotechnology, ceramics and electronics. Its R & D budget in 1983 corresponded to 3 per cent of sales (having risen sharply from 2.2 per cent over the previous five years), while a further 4 per cent was spent on technical design and development activity. Substantial efforts are devoted to monitoring research (particularly abroad) and forecasting emerging technological areas, the company being an enthusiastic user of MITI, STA and industrial research association forecasts. It not only operates an R & D Planning Department (with twenty personnel), but also an Office for Strategic Planning of R & D (consisting of six senior staff) whose task is to liaise with MITI, the STA and industrial associations. Each year, the company produces separate short-term (up to three years), medium-term (three to five years), and long-term (up to ten years) R & D plans. The planning process is complex, involving the integration of all the main corporate functions (production, sales, marketing, strategic planning and R & D). Besides the R & D Planning Department, the principal task of which is to identify key new technologies, a central role is played by an annual 'research managers' conference'. This was regarded as extremely important by those interviewed in that it enables all the firm's seventy R & D managers to meet for three days to discuss in depth the desirable shape of the corporate medium- and long-term research strategy. In 1982, for example, the conference was instrumental in establishing research projects in new fibres, biotechnology and electronics.

As in the electronics sector, it is clear that chemical firms, rather than MITI officials, have been primarily responsible for the composition of those elements of recent state-funded research programmes relevant to their interests (such as new polymers). In the case of the 'Basic Technologies for Future Industries' programme, one of the two companies visited described at length the origin of one of the component projects. Discussion first began within an informal group (described as a 'private organisation') consisting of the main chemical companies and well known academics. They were aware of the possibility of a new MITI initiative, and, in the space of a few meetings, were able to agree long-term priorities for the area and propose a number of possible projects. MITI then set up an 'official' working group (with virtually the same membership). This subsequently recommended a research programme which inevitably bore a close resemblance to the original ideas of the informal group, and which was therefore readily acceptable to industry. While perhaps smacking of 'corporatism', this close symbiosis of state and industry does seem capable of producing a portfolio of long-term research programmes in a manner which avoids the usual problem of government funds being used essentially to subsidise short-term R & D that firms would have undertaken anyway.

6.6 Forecasting of strategic and applied research: consultancy organisations

Among all the industrialised nations, Japan has perhaps the most extensive network of consultancy organisations, many of them extremely professional in their approach. These 'think-tanks' undertake an enormous variety of forecasting studies, covering trends in R & D across all major industrial sectors. In carrying out such forecasts, they are able to draw upon comprehensive and long-established data bases[24] developed over previous decades to monitor research activities abroad (especially in the United States) so that any promising areas of new work could be quickly identified and imported. This experience with developing systematic and rigorous approaches to monitoring R & D has proved invaluable in meeting the increasing demand, from the 1970s onwards, for longer-term technological forecasts. Most impressive, however, are the techniques that have been developed for what the less charitable might term low-level (but legal) industrial espionage, but which the Japanese prefer to describe as 'holistic', observational scanning of state-of-the-art industrial information' (private correspondence, 1984).

Major conventions and trade-fairs, particularly that at Hanover

which one interviewee described as the 'birthplace' of many important new technologies, are comprehensively and systematically
exploited for the very latest information on what overseas companies are doing and thinking. The following comments reveal this
clearly:

Trade fairs are very important for leading technological areas, and leading-edge
technological innovations. You can sometimes find demonstrations of important prototypes which have not yet been commercialised. There we find out
state-of-the-art technological 'seeds', many incidentally produced by UK companies. The sales-people at the fairs are often only too willing to tell us in
detail what they are doing . . . In particular, we go to the Hanover Trade Fair.
Every single booth is visited, discussions are held and all the technical literature
is collected. Afterwards, it is all carefully analysed, digested and stored. This
organisation regards this as a very important part of our work; it is a crucial
methodology. We in fact send a 50-person private study mission to Hanover.
[Interview, 1983.]

Among the Japanese consultancies visited were the Nomura Research
Institute (founded in 1965) and the Mitsubishi Research Institute
(established in 1970). These are the two largest technical consultancy
organisations, each with an annual turnover of over $40 million and
employing some 500 staff. They carry out a variety of longer-term
technological forecasts, analysing both changing market-demand and
research trends, and make use of all the traditional techniques (such
as scenario-analysis, trend-extrapolation and Delphi approaches).
Although it was not possible to obtain full details (due to problems
of confidentiality), the lists of completed projects include studies
of (a) relatively broad technological areas (perhaps of several sectors),
mainly for government agencies;[25] (b) individual sectors for industrial associations; (c) multi-client studies of a sector or sub-sector;
and (d) more specific studies (for example, on the prospects for
a new generation of products) for individual companies. The existence of this hierarchy of forecasts focusing on three different
levels (the national economy, industrial sectors and product areas)
is extremely important in that a forecast aimed at one level benefits
considerably from the existence of forecasts at the other two. For
example, a forecast focused on a particular sector can draw upon
and synthesise the results of more specific forecasts, while the
macro-level forecasts enable the relative significance of the sector,
and technological developments within it, to be seen in clearer light.
Indeed, one could claim that, without the significant forecasting
activities undertaken by industrial associations and companies,
the macro-level forecasts by government agencies would lose much
of their utility.

This and some of the other main lessons from Japan are discussed further in the next chapter along with the principal conclusions emerging from the reviews of forecasting in France, West Germany and the United States.

Notes

1. Because STA is responsible both for carrying out R & D and for overall co-ordination, this has led to accusations by other ministries of a certain conflict of interest. Furthermore, the roles of Monbusho, STA and MITI overlap appreciably, which has resulted in competition and even some conflict over control of new initiatives in strategic research.
2. A useful English-language summary of the university-based research system in Japan is given in Monbusho (1983). For details of the overall Japanese R & D system, including budgetary information, see STA (1982b).
3. According to both industrialists and officials in other government agencies, little attempt is made to assess even existing university research. The result is that much of it is apparently low in quality (a point made in STA, 1982b, ch. 1).
4. The newly set up 'Special Co-ordination Funds for Promoting Science and Technology' have a similar purpose (see note 7, below).
5. That this figure is so high is largely because an imputed figure of 50 per cent of academic salaries is attributed to research. Direct expenditure on research is less than 10 per cent of the overall total.
6. An evaluation was recently made of the 1970 STA forecast. Over the first ten of the thirty years considered in that study, the predictions were claimed to have an accuracy of over 60 per cent (interview with STA, 1983). The main type of error reported was that many of the predictions proved too conservative—in several areas the technology developed much faster than predicted. One explanation given for this was that certain industrial researchers attempted to obscure how far they had progressed in their R & D by deliberately over-stating the time needed to attain the objectives asked about in the forecast.
7. This was the main theme of the STA 'White Paper on Science and Technology 1982' (STA, 1982b), which was in fact subtitled 'In Pursuit of Creativity in Science and Technology'. The White Paper also described the establishment in 1981 of another programme ('Special Coordination Funds for Promoting Science and Technology', responsibility for which lies with the Council for Science and Technology). The aim of this programme is to co-ordinate and promote research activities vital to the development of science and technology in Japan. This programme has given particular priority to research projects in three fields: (a) life sciences; (b) materials science and technology; and (c) science and technology dealing with extreme conditions (for instance, research on superconductivity and cryogenics). Further details can be found in STA (1984, p. 37).
8. In order to minimise the risk of the research assuming a permanent character,

it is being carried out in space rented in existing laboratories rather than in newly created centres. Moreover, the research staff are only temporarily seconded from their parent institutions for the duration of projects, preference being given to young researchers (under 35 years old).

9. The Agency also supports experimental research programmes in its sixteen institutes.

10. The programme of twelve projects is being carried out by five research associations (made of up fifty industrial enterprises) in collaboration with ten government research institutes and universities. The ten years that the programme is scheduled to operate have been divided into three stages, with targets being set for each. In the first stage, several different approaches are being pursued in individual projects. At the end of that stage, progress is assessed by a project-evaluation committee whose task is to select the most promising approach for completing the project. This pluralist approach has been adopted to minimise the risk of overall failure, as well as to reduce the initial rivalry between the big companies over the control of the collaborations. By March 1984, the programme had already resulted in 435 patent applications, about 30 per cent of which are in the area of three-dimensional integrated circuits (*Japan Economic Journal*, 1984, p. 13).

11. To assist in preparing the report, the Industrial Structure Council set up a large drafting committee comprising some forty industrialists, academics and others.

12. The *1970s' Vision* was subsequently updated several times during the 1970s (see, for example, MITI, 1978).

13. As the report noted, 'In the past, Japanese industry achieved brilliant results in improving and applying imported technologies. In the '80s, however, it will be essential for Japan to develop technologies of its own' (MITI, 1980b, p. 16).

14. An interim report which contained all the main conclusions had, however, already been completed by late summer, 1980.

15. It is a little surprising that so eminent a Japanese commentator as Dore (1983) should give such great emphasis to a MITI-centred version of events, while almost ignoring the views of firms as to how the priorities were really arrived at (see the following sections for details of the latter). This is perhaps because he carried out no interviews with industry in the fieldwork for his report.

16. Moritani (1983, table 1.2, p. 5) reports that average increases in R & D spending by the ten largest Japanese corporations have been 125 per cent over the five years up to 1983.

17. Although it was not one of the companies visited, Mitsubishi Electric Corporation has attempted to formalise its approach to research forecasting more than most. It has, for example, devised a quantitative method for determining the relative priority of competing R & D projects—see Yanagishita (1984) for details.

18. It is interesting that Yamauchi (1983, p. 328), in his analysis of the development of long-range planning in Japanese R & D, suggests that 'roughly

speaking, before the 1970s, and especially before the 1973 oil crisis, the big Japanese companies failed to grasp the concept of corporate strategy and strategic R&D planning.'

19. For example, Company I regularly commissions studies from the Nomura Research Institute and other consultancies on their competitors' research profiles and patenting activities.

20. Company I sponsors over a hundred research projects at Japanese universities, and has endowed a chair at MIT. As with Company H, the aim is not so much to obtain research results of direct relevance to the firm as to promote a broad exchange of information, thereby keeping R & D staff fully up to date with the latest research developments around the world.

21. For example, it is planned that the longer-term research undertaken at Company J's Central Research Laboratory should double in the near future from 10 per cent to 20 per cent of the laboratory's overall effort.

22. The researchers involved claimed to be reasonably confident about their results, noting that the main problem was likely to be one of conservatism. Clearly, other firms are unlikely to reveal fully to Company J the details of their long-term plans, so some responses will inevitably be adjusted to suggest that the development-targets will be achieved later than actually expected.

23. Useful recent summaries of the rapid development of biotechnology and the life-sciences in Japan are given in JETRO (n.d.) and STA (1983b).

24. For example, there exist excellent information-scanning systems covering research journals, abstracts, conferences and patents, the information being available to subscribers on-line. In many cases, these data bases parallel those existing in Western Europe and the US (which Japan also uses), although for strategic research they are probably rather more comprehensive than those in the West.

25. Among the more global forecasts recently completed by the Mitsubishi Research Institute were two entitled 'Breakthrough Technology '90' and 'A Study of Technological Seeds Forming the Nucleus of Future Technical Developments'.

References

AIST (1981a), *Toward New Research and Development*, report of the Study Meeting for the Formulation of a Long-Term Industrial Technology Development Program, Agency of Industrial Science and Technology, Tokyo, MITI.

AIST (1981b), *Research and Development Project of Basic Technology for Future Industries*, Agency of Industrial Science and Technology, Tokyo, MITI.

AIST (1982a), *AIST 1982*, Agency of Industrial Science and Technology, Ministry of International Trade and Industry, Tokyo, MITI.

AIST (1982b), 'Research Development Project of Basic Technologies for Future Industries', *The Japanese Industrial and Technological Bulletin* (JETRO) **10**, November, pp. 4–10.

Dore, R. (1983), *A Case Study of Technology Forecasting in Japan*, London, Technical Change Centre.

Japan Economic Journal (1984), 'Next-generation fundamental technology R & D program—patent applications reach 435 under government-industry project', *The Japan Economic Journal*, 20 March, p. 13.

JETRO (n.d.), 'Research on biotechnology in Japan', mimeo, Tokyo, Japan External Trade Organisation.

LTCB (1983a), *Japan's High Technology Industries*, a report of the Industrial Research Division of the Long-Term Credit Bank of Japan, Ltd., Tokyo, Long-Term Credit Bank of Japan.

LTCB (1983b), 'Japan's high-tech industry', mimeo, Tokyo, Long-Term Credit Bank of Japan.

MITI (1978), *Japan's Industrial Structure—A Long Range Vision, 1978 Edition*, report of the Industrial Structure Council, Ministry of International Trade and Industry, Tokyo, MITI.

MITI (1980a), *The Vision of MITI Policies in the 1980s*, report of the Industrial Structure Council, Ministry of International Trade and Industry, Tokyo, MITI.

MITI (1980b), *The Vision of MITI Policies in the 1980s—Summary*, a summary version of MITI (1980a), Tokyo, MITI.

Monbusho (1983), *An Outline of the University-Based Research System in Japan*, Tokyo, Ministry of Education, Science and Culture.

Moritani, M. (1983), *Advanced Technology and the Japanese Contribution*, Tokyo, Nomura Securities Company.

STA (1972), *Science and Technology Developments up to AD 2000*, Science and Technology Agency, Tokyo, Japan Techno-Economics Society.

STA (1976), *Science and Technology Developments up to A.D. 2005*, Tokyo, Science and Technology Agency (in Japanese only).

STA (1982a), *Technology Development Forecast up to 2010*, Tokyo, Science and Technology Agency (in Japanese). An English summary can be found in *Science and Technology in Japan*, April/June 1983, pp. 24–9.

STA (1982b), *White Paper on Science and Technology 1982*, Tokyo, Science and Technology Agency (in Japanese). It was reproduced in English as *Japan Science and Technology Outlook*, Tokyo, Fuji Corporation, 1983.

STA (1983a), 'Exploratory Research for Advanced Technology (ERATO)', *Science and Technology in Japan*, January/March, pp. 21–3.

STA (1983b), 'Research and development of life sciences in Japan', *Science and Technology in Japan*, April/June, pp. 8–16.

STA (1984), ' "Special Coordination Funds for Promoting Science and Technology" projects set for FY 1985', *Science and Technology in Japan*, January/March, pp. 37–8.

Yamauchi, I. (1983), 'Long-range strategic planning in Japanese R & D', *Futures*, October, pp. 328–41.

Yanagishita, K. (1984), 'Soft science in Japan—ten years' experience in Mitsubishi Electric Corporation', pp. 239–331 in H. Eto and K. Matsui (eds), *R & D Management Systems in Japanese Industry*, Amsterdam, Elsevier Science Publishers, North-Holland.

7 Learning from others: cross-national comparisons

7.1 Introduction

The purpose of this chapter is two-fold. First, it summarises and contrasts the experiences with foresight activities in France, Japan, the United States and West Germany. Secondly, and perhaps more importantly, it examines the reasons behind the varying degrees of success achieved with these activities in the four countries, exploring more analytically the factors underlying the relative success and failure of the main forecasting initiatives discussed in previous chapters.

As far as possible, the structure of this chapter follows that adopted in the four country case-studies. We look first at the experience of national research-funding agencies with attempts to identify promising areas of basic science. This is followed by a discussion of the forecasting activities of ministries and departments responsible for the support of strategic and more applied research, comparisons also being made of the macro-level forecasting studies carried out by government agencies responsible for the overall co-ordination of national R & D efforts. Finally, we examine the experience of firms with longer-term research forecasting, noting the factors that appear to structure success and failure in such activities.

7.2 Lessons from national research-funding agencies

Of the four countries visited, arguably the lowest level of foresight activities within national research-funding agencies was encountered in West Germany,[1] with the Deutsche Forschungsgemeinschaft (DFG) and Max-Planck-Gesellschaft (MPG) both having made very little use of long-term forecasts in the past. Instead, as we saw in Chapter 4, decisions on funding priorities are reached using the traditional mechanism of expert committees and peer-review. The emphasis in such decisions has predominantly been on assessing future scientific opportunities rather than likely economic and technological benefits. When the DFG did attempt in the early 1970s to systematise its procedure for arriving at priorities through the use of questionnaires, the approach proved rather unsuccessful. The generally low level of foresight activities in the DFG and MPG was seen as reflecting the widely held belief in West Germany that basic research should not be directed centrally and that initiatives over new lines of research should be left to the scientific community— a reaction in part to the excesses associated with R & D planning by government during the Nazi period. This said, clear signs were evident during interviews with senior officials of a growing recognition of the limitations of peer-review as a policy-making mechanism, especially in relation to newly emerging research fields (where there are often no peers who can be consulted for advice), and more generally because of problems experienced in setting inter-field priorities.

In France and the United States, the Centre Nationale de la Recherche Scientifique (CNRS) and the National Science Foundation (NSF) were seen to have placed slightly more emphasis on long-term forecasting, primarily in the form of field surveys. From a comparative viewpoint, there are close similiarities between, in particular, the CNRS survey of solid-state physics and the early COSPUP studies (carried out under the aegis of the National Academy of Sciences, primarily with funds from NSF and other government agencies with responsibilities for basic research) in that both were carried out by expert groups in which industry was poorly represented, and little or no use was made of formal forecasting techniques. As we noted earlier, such surveys certainly served a number of useful purposes, including forcing researchers to think more systematically about the future and confronting them with policy issues. However, against these must be set the drawbacks with the approach adopted in the surveys, most importantly that it failed to take account of the likely technological, economic and social impacts of the research under review, that it proved largely incapable of yielding any overall set of funding priorities, and that it was intrinsically more suitable for established than newly emerging fields of science.

In some of the field surveys carried out in the 1970s, an attempt was made to remedy these problems. Thus, in both the CNRS study on atomic and molecular physics and the Bromley Report on Physics, a more structured approach was adopted in assessing future scientific prospects, although like earlier surveys they continued to give little consideration to demand-side factors. In contrast, the Hugo Report on Energy Sources took account of such external factors but it made no use of formal forecasting techniques. The only field survey examined that combined 'science-push' and 'demand-pull' perspectives *and* adopted a more formal approach (in this case, through the use of a systematic ranking exercise undertaken by postal question-naire) was the Cohen Report on Materials Science. It is perhaps not coincidental that this COSPUP report was one of the more success-ful of the field surveys carried out in the 1960s and 1970s.

However, the adoption of a 'two-sided' approach to forecasting and the use of more systematic techniques by no means guarantees the success of attempts to identify strategically important areas of basic research. This was only too clear from our analysis of the NSF's experience in the late 1970s with three reports commissioned from consultancies. In the Arthur D. Little study, 'relevance trees' were used to link basic research to industrial objectives and techno-logical options. However, because the study was carried out by professional forecasters without adequately surveying the views of practising scientists, the resultant priorities identified for basic research were too general to be operationally useful to the NSF. The Battelle study likewise attempted to relate industrial needs to scientific opportunities and again produced no more than the most general of predictions, many of which subsequently proved to be mistaken. The lesson from these two exercises is that the adoption of formal forecasting techniques in foresight activities must not be at the expense of failing to involve the relevant research com-munities, if only to ensure that some sense of commitment to the results of the forecast is generated. Without the support of the scientific community, forecasts produced by 'outsider' consultancies stand little chance of being implemented in policy. Given the recent development of certain promising techniques for identifying newly emerging research areas (for example, those being pioneered by CHI Research), officials in research-funding agencies might be tempted to believe that they offer a simpler and more reliable way to arrive at priorities than traditional peer-review procedures, and that exten-sive consultation with the research community is no longer neces-sary. The experience of the NSF shows that such a temptation must be resisted.

In the light of the above comments, the French initiative in setting up an in-house forecasting group (CEP) within CNRS is especially interesting. The CNRS 'clubs' have been able, through extensive involvement of industrial researchers, to ensure that external criteria are taken into account alongside internal scientific ones, but they have previously lacked the detailed information needed to approach their task systematically. Now that CEP has begun to develop data bases relevant to long-term forecasting, there are good grounds for believing that the resulting information will complement and signifi-cantly improve the decision-making process within CNRS.

From an overall perspective, the experience of national research-funding agencies suggests that attempts to identify strategically promising areas of science which are based on a one-sided approach (focusing on scientific opportunities to the exclusion of 'demand-side' factors, or vice versa), or which are carried out solely using expert-committee procedures, are unlikely to prove successful. The prospects are somewhat better if formal forecasting techniques are also employed, or if a two-sided approach (i.e. balancing 'science-push' against 'demand-pull' considerations) is adopted. However, by far the most effective approach is to combine both, while at the same time ensuring that the relevant research community is fully involved in the exercise—a lesson which emerges equally forcibly from a consideration of the respective experiences with research forecasting of government departments and agencies.

7.3 Lessons from government departments, ministries and agencies[2]

Compared to national research-funding agencies which have tended to carry out forecasts of a 'field-survey' type, far greater diversity in approach was evident among government bodies responsible for supporting strategic and applied research or for overall co-ordination of R & D activities. We look first at the experience of these bodies with field surveys, and then at some of the other longer-term forecasting approaches used in the four countries.

Longer-term surveys of specific fields have, as we have seen, occasionally been carried out by the Ministry of Industry and Research (MIR) in France (for example, on telecommunications and information technology) and by the Federal Ministry of Research and Technology (BMFT) in West Germany (on materials science, for instance). These studies were carried out largely on the basis of consultations with experts in the relevant research communities, with no attempt being made to employ formal forecasting techniques. Consequently, they suffered from many of the failings of similar field surveys undertaken by national research-funding agencies, in particular the tendency to concentrate more on scientific opportunities than economic and social needs. Some attempt to address this problem has been made in the 'Research Briefings' recently initiated in the United States (by the Office of Science and Technology Policy) through ensuring a higher level of industrial representation on the panels responsible for their preparation; and in the case of the ERAB forecasting exercise by the US Department of Energy (DoE), not only was industry well represented on the survey panel, but a more systematic approach to arriving at research priorities was also employed. The fact that the ERAB exercise proved among the more successful of these various surveys reinforces the lesson drawn at the end of the previous section.

Besides field surveys, the ministries and agencies visited have also commissioned various forecasts from consultancies. Some of these have not been particularly successful—for example, the SRI/Chase study for the DoE, the search for 'white spots' initiated by BMFT and several studies by the Institute for Systems Technology and Innovation Research for the Fraunhofer-Gesellschaft. Again, a key problem appears to have been the inability of the forecasters to integrate their efforts effectively with established research-policy procedures. The crucial importance of ensuring that forecasting addresses concrete policy issues has been most clearly recognised in Japan, and more recently in France. In the latter, the rationale behind setting up the Centre de Prospective et d'Evaluation (CPE) and the Centre d'Etudes des Systèmes et des Technologies Avancées (CESTA) was precisely to bring professional forecasters into contact both with policy-makers and with researchers seconded to MIR to run its research programmes, and to provide more systematic information relevant to decision-making. In other words, the aim is to supplement rather than replace the traditional peer-review process. Similar thinking underlies the extensive use of commissioned forecasts as an input into decision-making by the Science and Technology Agency (STA) and Ministry of International Trade and Industry (MITI) in Japan.

A third type of approach to foresight activities is represented by the *Five-Year Outlooks* in the United States, which constituted an attempt to avoid the problems associated with the use of field-surveys. However, once this initiative had been 'captured' by the basic research community, the *Outlooks* fell victim to many of the same failings as the earlier COSPUP studies, in particular the comparative neglect of demand-side considerations and the inability to establish overall priorities. The clear lesson here is that the task of identifying national basic research priorities cannot be devolved to the scientific community in the shape of its professional organisations and learned societies.

However, undoubtedly the most important lessons came from the fourth type of approach to long-term forecasting—the macro-level initiatives represented by the 'National Colloquium' and 'Technology Consultations' in France, and the STA thirty-year forecasts and MITI 'visions' in Japan. What both countries have recognised is that foresight activities must go beyond just identifying new research areas of long-term significance and ensure that researchers and policy-makers in industry, government and elsewhere then act upon the results of the forecasts. The best way of achieving this is to involve large sections of these communities in the forecasting process itself. As a result, even though the National Colloquium held in France does not in retrospect appear to have constituted a particularly systematic approach to identifying promising areas of science, it did succeed in generating a level of consensus necessary to translate the results of the exercise into policy. The same is true of the Technology Consultations, the STA forecasts and the MITI 'visions', all of which adopted a rather more systematic approach. In drawing detailed conclusions, we shall, however, concentrate on the Japanese exercises because the first Technology Consultation was in comparison only a small-scale effort, while it is at the time of writing too soon to judge the full impact of the second.

There are perhaps five main lessons that can be learned from the STA and MITI experiences with strategic research forecasting. The first is that, to stand any real chance of success, attempts to identify areas of basic research having long-term strategic importance need to be informed by up-to-date background information on research trends throughout the world's main industrial nations, and covering academic, government and industrial research sectors. During the post-war period when Japan was pursuing a strategy of closing the 'technology gap' with the United States and Western Europe, government agencies (and firms, as we note below) developed rigorous techniques for monitoring research activities world-wide and compiling readily accessible data banks. These have subsequently proved invaluable as the focus of monitoring has switched from applied research and technological development to strategic research, and as the associated need for longer-term foresight activities has grown.

Secondly, as has been stressed previously, the reliable identification of emerging areas of strategic research is greatly facilitated by adopting an approach that fully integrates 'science-push' and 'demand-pull' perspectives. This relates to one of the principal conclusions of Chapter 2—that successful innovation normally depends on coupling scientific and technological advances with changed market demands. Consequently, attempts to foresee the likely impact of science on commercially important technological fields cannot ignore these two crucial aspects of the innovation process. In Japan, it has been found by STA that the best way to achieve this synthesis is to involve large numbers of active researchers (to a great extent, regardless of their seniority) from academia and government laboratories on the one hand, and from industry on the other. Because of the structure of science-based companies in Japan (and in particular the generally good communication that exists between R & D departments and other corporate functions), industrial researchers often have the clearest views on probable technological developments and likely product-lines and markets for them. As a result, they are in a strong position to help determine field-by-field priorities not only for state-funded industrial research, but also for strategic research carried out in universities and government laboratories.

Related to this is a third lesson—the advantages of adopting a 'bottom-up' approach to forecasting rather than the centralised 'top-down' approach often favoured by government. Thus, MITI 'taps into' the long-term planning and forecasting work already being carried out by firms—either individually or collectively through industrial associations—and provides a framework for the coordination of these various 'visions', rather than attempting to impose views and priorities from above. Apart from being dependent on a narrower range of information inputs, 'top-down' forecasts and the resultant research policies are more likely to antagonise not only the basic science community (which may feel that it has been inadequately consulted in the foresight process), but also industry (which naturally tends to feel that it is in the best position to judge the commercial prospects for strategic research). By integrating wide range of interests into the process for establishing priorities, the Japanese approach by and large avoids the danger of alienating these two vital constituencies while at the same time minimising the lack of appreciation of current scientific and technological concerns often associated with centrally determined R & D plans.

This leads to a fourth general lesson concerning strategic research forecasting—that the role of government ministries and agencies should be confined to the identification of broad trends only (as, for example, in the STA forecasts), leaving industrial associations and individual firms to carry out more specific forecasts relating to the identification of new products and processes and the markets for them. Information on overall trends is generally sufficient for the purposes of government, provided that the range of research activities surveyed is sufficiently broad to permit a 'holistic' overview to be obtained (i.e. the forecasts are not based on individual, discipline-based 'fields'). Information at such a level of aggregation can, for example, help government agencies identify newly emerging interdisciplinary fields where two or more previously separate lines of research have merged. MITI and STA are therefore well placed to decide which basic technologies are still in the pre-competitive phase of development, and to identify and prioritise those areas of basic research upon which the technologies will draw. Decisions over proposed programmes and projects within particular fields can then be judged competitively in the normal way, with the relevant research communities determining detailed lower-level priorities.

The last and arguably the most valuable lesson from the STA and MITI forecasts is that the main benefit of such exercises is not so much the specific forecasts they yield—those interviewed in Japan were on the whole remarkably uninterested in the accuracy of past predictions.[3] Rather, their importance lies in the *process* by which the forecasts are generated. A number of distinct aspects to this can be identified: (a) bringing together disparate groups of people (academics, industrial researchers from different sectors, policy-makers, professional forecasters and scientific commentators), and providing a structure within which they can communicate directly or indirectly (through a Delphi-style forecast) with each other; (b) forcing them periodically to concentrate seriously and systematically on the longer-term future; (c) enabling them to co-ordinate their future R & D activities; (d) creating a measure of consensus on future priorities for strategic research; and (e) most importantly, generating a feeling of *commitment* to the results of the forecasts, so that the predictions made are likely to become largely self-fulfilling—as one of those interviewed put it, 'it is important to realise that forecasts can in a very real sense create the future'. It is these five aspects of the forecasting process—communication, concentration on the future, co-ordination, creation of consensus, and commitment—that are recognised by the Japanese as constituting the key benefits of their approach to longer-term foresight activities. These benefits have been seen, at least until now, as substantially outweighing any of the disadvantages associated with the approach—in particular, its inherent tendencies (discussed in section 6.3.2) towards conservatism and encouraging excessive competition on the basis of a restricted range of technological options. Whether this continues to hold true in the future as the Japanese place increasing emphasis on more basic research (where creativity and unconventional approaches are clearly at a premium) remains to be seen.

7.4 Lessons from industry

On the whole, we found considerably greater uniformity among companies' experience with foresight activities in the four countries visited than was the case with research-funding agencies and government departments. None the less, significant differences exist in the approaches used by firms to identify strategically important research areas. Analysis of the strengths and weaknesses of the various approaches leads to five principal lessons which to a great extent reinforce those already drawn.

The first is the appreciation by most firms (and especially those in Japan) that, to succeed in long-term research forecasting, extensive efforts must be devoted to world-wide monitoring of relevant R & D activities. This typically covers work underway in university departments, government research institutes, and, wherever possible, the laboratories of industrial competitors. Such monitoring involves not only systematic scanning of written material (academic journals, technical literature, trade journals, patents etc.) but also the use of links developed with the basic research community—for example, through retaining an international network of senior academic consultants or commissioning research projects in universities and government-supported research institutes. As we saw in section 6.6, Japanese consultancy organisations are at the forefront in terms of state-of-the-art approaches to R & D monitoring, and their expertise is sought not only by Japanese industry but also increasingly by Western companies.

Secondly, the firms that have been most successful in their foresight activities are those that have explicitly recognised the need to adopt a two-sided approach whereby 'science-push' opportunities are balanced against likely changes in market demand (see the discussion of the differing experiences of Companies E and G in the United States contained in section 5.5). This is generally achieved by ensuring that staff from all corporate functions (including strategic planning, production engineering, sales and marketing) are from the outset fully involved, along with researchers, in all major foresight exercises. In addition to adopting a two-sided approach, many firms have also recognised that a structured approach drawing upon formal forecasting techniques is more likely to prove successful than one based solely on group discussions and informal soundings within the company (the experiences of Company G are again particularly instructive). In this respect, it is by no means essential for firms to have high-level professional forecasting expertise in-house; some firms rely primarily on outside consultancy organisations to provide the necessary skills, while others believe there are significant benefits to be gained from establishing a specialised group within the firm to carry out at least the more company-specific forecasts (of individual technologies and product-lines) even if sector-wide studies continue to be commissioned from outside.

A third lesson is that, as with MITI 'visions', greater success is likely to be achieved with forecasts that adopt a 'bottom-up' approach based on wide participation by company employees. Thus, the more successful foresight activities generally involve bringing together large numbers of staff from the research division and other corporate functions, perhaps with the assistance of professional forecasters, to identify systematically promising research opportunities. This may then be followed by more detailed forecasts relating to the particular technology areas involved and the strategic research that will feed into them. Because such an approach provides a mechanism for 'tapping into' the wide range of potentially innovative ideas often held by staff in disparate parts of the company, the results it yields are more likely to prove successful than those generated by centralised 'top-down' foresight activities.

Fourthly, many companies, not just in Japan, have come to recognise that the *process* involved in identifying promising lines of research can be as important as the actual results of the forecast themselves. The reasons are similar to those discussed previously in relation to government departments, i.e. the forecasting exercises stimulate communication between different parts of the company, they encourage people to concentrate more on the longer-term future than would otherwise be the case, they provide a mechanism for co-ordinating R & D activities throughout the company (for example, between the various divisional R & D laboratories and the central research laboratory), they help create consensus on priorities, and they generate a sense of commitment to the resulting corporate R & D policy.

The final lesson we shall draw relates to the fact that the experiences with foresight activities of companies in France, West Germany and the United States have been appreciably more mixed than those in Japan. This is despite the fact that the approach to longer-term forecasting adopted by Western firms has often not been very different from that of Japanese companies. In our view, this suggests that even large firms cannot do everything on their own. Corporate research forecasting must be set in a wider context, and the overall framework can only be provided by the state. Experiences in Japan suggest that foresight activities need to be conducted simultaneously at three main levels, with the results from each feeding into the forecasting efforts at the two other levels. The three levels are:

(a) macro-level forecasts of the type carried out by STA and MITI;
(b) sector-level forecasts—for example, those carried out by industrial associations, or multi-client studies by consultancy organisations;

(c) more specific research forecasts relating to particular technologies or new product-lines.

If one or more of these elements is missing (as they often are in
France, West Germany and the United States), then the remaining
elements are likely to be less successful. The results of our study
suggest that, outside Japan, the main problem associated with
longer-term foresight activities stems from the absence or relative
weakness of forecasting at level (a), and, to a lesser extent level (b).
How nations might set about remedying this is the subject of the
final chapter.

Notes

1. As was seen in Chapter 6, there is no separate national research-funding
   agency for basic research in Japan, the nearest equivalent being Monbusho.
   In the past, Monbusho has made very little attempt to set priorities centrally,
   and has therefore not resorted to longer-term forecasting activities. Only
   recently has the Ministry begun to carry out field surveys similar to those
   undertaken in other countries.
2. Even though not a 'government' agency, we include the Fraunhofer-Gesellschaft in our discussion here because of its responsibilities for strategic and
   applied research.
3. The usual answer to any question on this subject in the course of our interviews was a smile, followed by a joke along the lines of, 'it is just like you
   British to ask such a question—you are always looking to the past. In Japan,
   we think only about the future!'

8 Conclusions: future options for picking scientific winners

8.1 Approaches to research forecasting: a summary

Our main aim in this final chapter is to draw overall conclusions as to the most promising options available to government for picking future 'scientific winners'. This entails consideration not just of the methods for identifying promising areas of science, but also of the institutional procedures and responsibilities required for their successful implementation—for example, the respective roles of government departments, research-funding agencies, industry and the scientific community (including its professional organisations). Although we concentrate on setting out some suggestions as to how Britain in particular might best develop its longer-term foresight activities, our proposals do, we shall argue, also have some general relevance to the problems currently facing many Western countries.

We began in the first chapter by explaining how the development of new technology-based industries has resulted in additional demands being placed on the state-funded infrastructure for R & D. A significant part of the basic research underway in academic and government establishments has begun to acquire increased strategic importance, while at the same time firms in certain industrial sectors now see the need to undertake appreciably more basic research. The latter clearly has implications for the type of R & D support that the state should provide, with funding for large-scale 'collective research' programmes relating to new basic technologies assuming greater significance. Governments have therefore begun to find themselves having to make new choices as to how to allocate the resources available for research. One question that is now assuming particular prominence is whether it is possible to identify accurately and at an early stage those newly emerging areas of strategic research that will provide the knowledge-base for the technologies and industries of tomorrow. Clearly, if targeted support can be made available promptly to academic, government and industrial research laboratories, this could constitute a particularly effective use of the inevitably limited government funds for R & D.

In subsequent chapters, we went on to explore the lessons that may be drawn from past experience with a variety of approaches to research forecasting. In Chapter 2, we first considered what can be learnt from retrospective analyses of the roles of curiosity-orientated science, strategic research and applied R & D in the innovation process. Although the lessons from history are by no means unambiguous, we were able to conclude that they provide some support for the viability of undertaking longer-term forecasting activities in relation to emerging areas of strategic research. In contrast, we concluded that the prediction of radical new break-throughs stemming from curiosity-orientated research is far less feasible, and is therefore probably not a worthwhile pursuit for governments or research-funding agencies.

This analysis of the interface between basic research and industrial R & D provided the theoretical background to the next four chapters which considered, in turn, experiences with research forecasting in France, West Germany, the United States and Japan, while Chapter 7 synthesised some general lessons about the techniques and pro-cedures most likely (or unlikely) to yield satisfactory results. The integration of 'science-push' and 'demand-pull' perspectives is, as we have seen, generally a prerequisite for success. Equally impor-tantly, although various formal forecasting techniques (along with specialised consultancy organisations) are now available, these should be used with caution. They must not be employed in isolation but integrated into a wider process involving the relevant research com-munities (in government, academia and industry) and addressing concrete and clearly formulated policy aims (such as informing decisions over the distribution of R & D funds). In addition, the previous chapter discussed the strengths and weaknesses of the different approaches used in the foresight exercises considered in our review—for example, the problems often encountered in surveys of specific fields of science based solely on the views of a narrow constituency of academic scientists. However, if there is one over-riding lesson that emerges from our study, it is the desirability of integrating, as the Japanese have done, the forecasting efforts of government, funding-agencies, and industry, something which can only be achieved by drawing in wide sections of the research com-munity.

On the basis of our findings, it would now be possible to put forward a set of guidelines as to how an individual ministry of industry or national science agency, for example, might most effec-tively attempt to improve its foresight efforts. That we have chosen not to do this is partly out of a desire to avoid repeating much of the detail contained in the last chapter, but more importantly because we feel it might divert attention from what is in our view the central problem confronting science-policy makers in most Western countries. This concerns the need to develop (a) the knowledge-base required to help determine overall priorities for publicly-funded strategic research, and (b) appropriate mechanisms for co-ordinating research in government laboratories and universities with infra-structural R & D support for industry. As we saw in Chapters 6 and 7, experience in Japan suggests that the crucial first step may well be to initiate macro-level forecasts of the type pioneered by the Science and Technology Agency. In the absence of the holistic over-view which they provide, isolated attempts to carry out longer-term strategic research forecasts—whether by research-funding agencies, individual government departments, industrial associations or firms —are likely to meet, at best, with mixed success.

In what follows, we discuss how one particular country, namely Britain, might set about engaging in a greater degree of macro-level forecasting, and describe some of the institutional implications involved. Although the focus is very much on Britain, most indus-trialised nations (apart from Japan) could in our view benefit substantially from increasing their foresight activities in the way described. Consequently, the options put forward should be of more general interest, at the same time as serving to illustrate in a concrete manner the types of action required.

It must be stressed at this point that, unlike what has gone before, much of what we have to say in this concluding chapter is necessarily a personal view. What follows is in no way intended to constitute a comprehensive set of recommendations. The proposals put forward are provisional ones and will no doubt be developed further through debate. We see their main function as providing no more than a framework for future discussion on these vital issues.

8.2 Macro-level strategic research forecasting: an option for Britain

If our views about research forecasting are in any way biased, this is almost certainly because of our experiences in Japan. While the interviews we undertook in France, West Germany and the United States on balance revealed considerable scepticism about the accuracy achievable in longer-term strategic forecasting, and indeed about the utility of such exercises, few such doubts were expressed in Japan. Officials in government agencies and firms alike were convinced that formal, detailed and extensive research forecasting is absolutely essential to continued economic progress. The reason for this belief is the almost universal acceptance that technological innovation constitutes a major (perhaps even the most important) determinant of continued economic and social progress. In this respect, it is worth restating part of the quotation from section 6.3.1 in which those responsible for the first Science and Technology Agency thirty-year forecast put their case so persuasively and unequivocally.

Science and technology are . . . *the* prime movers of our socioeconomic development now, and it would be no exaggeration to say that they will bring about *all* the major future growth and advances of the nation. In view of this . . . it is essential to formulate a long range plan . . . [for] science and technology . . . In framing such a plan, it is most important to foresee likely future socioeconomic changes and to pinpoint those branches of science and technology which will meet renewed requirements. [STA, 1972, p. 7, emphasis added.]

Even if one accepts only the general tenor of this Japanese view, then it follows that the difference in the level of scientific foresight activities between Japan and other industrialised nations revealed very clearly in this study must be seen as *one* of the factors (and clearly there are many others of significance) contributing to the country's markedly better performance over recent years in technology-based industrial sectors. (Particularly alarming evidence on the deteriorating technological position of European nations can be found in a recent survey reported in *The Wall Street Journal*, 1984.) Although the above Japanese view can be criticised for implying an excessive degree of technological determinism—it takes insufficient account, for example, of the extent to which deliberate political and social decisions should structure choices relating to the industrial and technological future—we do have some sympathy with the argument that a strong science-based economy is essential for industrialised countries whatever type of future is chosen as desirable. Hence, the main proposal that we offer can be stated very briefly: the United Kingdom (and probably most Western industrial nations as well) should attempt to bring its level of longer-term foresight activities up to that found in Japan. In our view, the key first step towards achieving this end involves the initiation of macro-level forecasting to inform overall government planning (especially in relation to the allocation of resources for strategic research) while at the same time aiding and encouraging industry to increase its own foresight activities.

However, while long-term forecasting may have a potentially valuable role to play in helping establish government policies for science and technology (including those relating to the provision of infrastructural support for industrial R & D), the possibilities that it will be carried out poorly or ineffectively are appreciable. This is amply demonstrated by the unsatisfactory experiences recorded in many of the agencies and organisations visited in the course of our study. Consequently, for the remainder of this chapter we shall assume the reader is prepared to accept our conclusion that the overall volume of macro-level foresight activity should be increased in the United Kingdom, and instead concentrate on attempting to map out an approach for achieving this that avoids the most serious pitfalls revealed by experience in other countries. We shall consider in turn a number of conditions that must be met if such long-term forecasting is to be both accurate and useful. These conditions can be divided into a number of categories relating to (a) the aims of the forecast, (b) the general nature of macro-level foresight activities by government, (c) the process for carrying out specific forecasts, and (d) putting foresight activities on a permanent and routine basis.

8.2.1 *The aims of macro-level forecasting*

The first condition is that the aims of any foresight activity must be clearly specified. Forecasts carried out without definite objectives will almost certainly have little or no impact, however accurate the predictions they may contain. In the case of Britain, we suggest three principal aims for centrally co-ordinated macro-level foresight activity.

(1) The planned research forecast should inform those concerned with the allocation of the government's 'Science Budget' (which is used to support most areas of academic research in Britain through grants disbursed by five Research Councils, as well as a number of Research Council laboratories—for details, see Ronayne, 1984, pp. 128–41), in particular those who have to decide on the distribution of funds between broad fields of science. The intention would be to provide the responsible body, the Advisory Board for the Research Councils (ABRC) and the relevant ministry (the Department of Education and Science, DES), with background information of assistance in developing a more holistic perspective on basic research, enabling them to see when particular fields are beginning to take on a strategic character. In this way, ABRC, DES, and the five Research Councils would be in a position to introduce external techno-logical and economic criteria to a greater extent into policy-making (while still preserving the requirement that detailed funding decisions on individual programmes and projects be

made primarily according to intrinsic scientific merit). Above all, it is essential to avoid a field-by-field approach to research forecasting, since this is almost certain to encounter problems similar to those associated with the COSPUP surveys and 'Research Briefings' undertaken in the United States (see Chapter 5).

(2) Another aim is that any such forecast should inform government ministries with responsibilities for funding strategic and applied industrial research about the possibilities for establishing co-operative research programmes likely to be central in developing new 'core' or 'generic' technologies. In Britain, the Department of Trade and Industry is particularly important because of the role of its various Requirements Boards in relation to strategic and applied industrial research, and because of its initiatives in new technological growth areas such as the 'Alvey Programme' on information technology.

(3) The final aim of centrally co-ordinated macro-level forecasting should be to popularise the notion of looking into the future, demonstrating that longer-term foresight activities are both possible and useful. The intention here would be to persuade policy-makers in ministries, research councils, firms and research associations, among others, of the benefits of such forecasts, thus encouraging them to build up their own foresight activities focusing on more specific issues. The latter has certainly been one of the long-term effects of the forecasts carried out by the Science and Technology Agency. Another benefit that we would also expect to result from an STA-type forecast as proposed here is the encouragement of better communication among industry, government and academia, with a resulting increase in the degree of consensus on national priorities for basic research. As noted at the end of section 7.3, the Japanese regard this function of macro-level foresight activities as no less important than the actual forecasts themselves.

8.2.2 *General nature of macro-level forecasting*

Having established the overall aims of our proposed forecasting initiative, let us now consider the format it should ideally take. There are six main aspects to this.

(1) Assuming that the initial forecasting exercise proves reasonably successful, subsequent forecasts need to be carried out *regularly*, perhaps every three to five years. This is essential given the rapid pace of advance witnessed in certain areas of research and technology over the last few years.

(2) The forecast should cover *all areas of research* so that a holistic perspective can be developed, thereby facilitating the early recognition of cross-field linkages and emerging areas of strategic research and basic technology. Forecasts focusing on individual fields, in contrast, too often tend to become dominated by existing vested interests, as we have seen in previous chapters. Furthermore, because they focus on institutionally defined 'fields' (the boundaries of which may no longer reflect current research practices), they frequently ignore newly developing interdisciplinary areas.

(3) Despite its wide scope, the forecast should be comparatively *inexpensive*. The experience of the Japanese Science and Technology Agency shows that very ambitious long-term forecasts can still be carried out relatively cheaply. In contrast, the fact that several of the more narrowly focused COSPUP field-surveys failed to meet this criterion of cheapness was one reason why they were widely criticised by the US policy-makers whom we interviewed.

(4) One very important condition is that those chosen to participate in the questionnaire surveys required in a forecast of the sort envisaged should not be 'delegates' representing institutions or research areas (a situation militating against the possibility of identifying inter-field priorities). Nor should they consist entirely of distinguished elder 'statesmen' of science at the tail-end of their careers. Rather they should primarily be chosen from among *active and highly regarded researchers* covering the full range of scientific fields and industrial sectors. As such, the forecast would essentially be a 'bottom-up' exercise, synthesising and integrating the views of knowledgeable experts in industry and gifted basic scientists who are often already engaged in informal monitoring and forecasting activities within their own individual spheres of interest. Again, the experience of the Science and Technology Agency suggests that about half should be drawn from industry, one-third from universities and government laboratories, while the remainder should include policy-makers, technological forecasters, science commentators and social scientists. Particular efforts should be made to ensure that younger researchers are well represented.

(5) Control of the forecasting exercise should not be handed over to professional consultants even though they may be brought in to assist with the survey. Nor for the reasons discussed in Chapter 7 should responsibility be devolved to the basic science community, in particular the national academy of sciences (the

Royal Society in the case of Britain), although it should clearly be involved. Because of the need to involve all ministries with significant R & D interests, macro-level forecasts must be organised centrally at a super-ministerial level. In Britain, this might entail overall co-ordination by the Cabinet Office, with strong participation by both ACARD (whose role is to provide independent advice to government on more applied research and development) and the ABRC. It could not be carried out solely by ACARD (the remit of which does not extend to many of the more basic areas of publicly funded research), while if responsibility were devolved to ABRC alone it would run the danger of suffering the same fate as the *Five-Year Outlooks* in the United States (see section 5.4).

(6) Finally, all those participating in the forecast need to be assured that their *views will be treated confidentially* and reported only in the form of aggregate statistics. Without such an assurance, industrial researchers in particular may feel it necessary to 'clear' their responses with senior management before submitting them, and as we saw in Chapter 6 this can lead to conservatively biased views about the future.

8.2.3 *Procedures for undertaking the macro-level forecast*

The third set of specifications relates to the actual process of carrying out the type of long-term research forecast advocated here, particularly the first time it is attempted. Again, the approach adopted in most Japanese forecasts provides a useful model. We would envisage the exercise proceeding in several stages. First, a competent working group (and not just a supervisory committee) needs to be set up, consisting of those who would actually be responsible for organising the study. The level of effort required is probably such that core members of the working group would need to be temporarily seconded from their present employment (in industry, government or academia) for a few months.

The next stage required can best be described as a systematic 'ransacking' exercise, gathering together on a world-wide basis the results generated by all recent forecasts (in particular, those by government departments and funding agencies in leading industrial nations). Major British science-based firms might even be persuaded to reveal (again on a confidential basis) the results of forecasts that they have recently commissioned or purchased as part of a multi-client package, as well as being approached to provide the working group with useful assistance on technological intelligence-gathering (for example, on major research programmes of long-term industrial significance underway in high-technology companies abroad).

On this basis, the working group would acquire the background information needed to proceed to the next stage of preparing the questionnaire to be used in the survey. It might, however, first be necessary to carry out a limited number of interviews with especially well-informed researchers (perhaps two or three for each of the main industrial sectors) in order to establish more precisely the issues on which the questionnaire should focus. In addition, a two-stage survey procedure would probably be required the first time the forecast was attempted, with a preliminary questionnaire being sent out containing relatively open-ended questions. The experts to whom it was sent would be asked to identify (a) current 'state-of-the-art' technologies in their industry (or, for academic and government researchers, the industrial sectors most likely to draw upon the results of their basic research); (b) possible new technologies in the sectors identified and the types of product group or production process on which they might impact; (c) areas of strategic research with some long-term potential relevance to the sector; and (d) the areas of more basic research that show promise of providing important inputs over coming years to the strategic research areas identified in (c). The results of this preliminary survey would then be used to compile a second questionnaire, the aim of which would be to obtain more detailed information on such questions as (i) the relative importance of different areas of strategic research (both existing and newly emerging); (ii) the likely time-scale before they begin to yield technological benefits; (iii) appropriate support mechanisms by which government (together with industry) might accelerate their development; and (iv) the competence of individual respondents to pass judgement on the particular research areas on which they have commented.

In order to cover the full range of scientific fields and industrial sectors adequately, the questionnaire should be sent to a large number of experts, in particular active industrial researchers, academics and research managers. Japanese experience suggests that at least a thousand responses would be required to ensure the necessary breadth of coverage, provided that sufficient care is taken to ensure representative sampling. As we have emphasised in several places earlier, this wide-ranging involvement of expert opinion would have the additional benefit of generating the level of commitment within the research community needed to ensure that the results of the forecast are integrated into subsequent decisions on research policy in both government and industry.

Finally, the overall results of the survey would be analysed and a preliminary report prepared. This should be circulated widely, with the resulting comments being used in the compilation of the final version for publication.

8.2.4 *Establishing macro-level forecasting on a continuing basis*

The final set of conditions we see as necessary for the success of our proposed forecasting initiative concerns the means by which such forecasts, once begun, can be organised successfully on a regular basis and be guaranteed to have a substantive impact on policy throughout the national R & D system. The first condition that needs to be met is the existence of detailed and up-to-date R & D statistics. Without such data, research forecasts stand little chance of being accurate. Unfortunately, despite having once been the world-leader in this field, Britain now has the dubious distinction of being among the industrialised nations with the least satisfactory statistics on research activity and output. The difference between Britain and Japan is especially marked. Whereas there is a delay of only twelve months or so before most Japanese data for the preceding year become available, in Britain the most recent statistical series have often tended to be two, three or even four years out of date.[1] Attempting to make predictions and decisions on such a basis obviously imposes a substantial and completely unnecessary handicap on policy-makers in Britain.

Similar considerations apply in relation to the coverage of R & D statistics. Clearly, longer-term forecasting requires several types of information, in particular comprehensive data on the inputs to research (whether carried out in firms, academia or government establishments), preferably in a form where valid comparisons can be drawn with other countries.[2] Regular statistics on important subjects, such as qualified practising scientists and engineers broken down by sector, have also been lacking in the United Kingdom over recent years. In addition, research forecasting requires output data, and this is another area where Britain needs to improve its efforts (for a review of the limited extent to which research evaluation is carried out in the UK, see Irvine, Martin and Oldham, 1983), perhaps exploring the approaches being pioneered by organisations such as CHI Research (see section 5.6). In particular, greater emphasis needs to be given to monitoring research activities abroad. In the past, perhaps because of a feeling that Britain was one of the world's scientific leaders and therefore had little to learn from others, only minimal attention was given to monitoring foreign research. Now that Britain undertakes only about 5 per cent of the world's scientific and technological activities, this previous neglect of monitoring must be rectified. (Indeed, besides monitoring research, there is also a need to keep abreast of the latest approaches to forecasting used in overseas countries, particularly Japan, the clear world-leader in this area.) In parallel with initiating macro-level research forecasting, government should in our view make it a priority to catalyse and support initiatives to develop more extensive indigenous data banks (on the scientific literature, patents, general technological information and so on) comparable to those existing in the United States and Japan.

Besides developing better R & D data, a second pressing requirement for setting longer-term research forecasting on to a permanent and routine basis is for government to promote the development of wide-ranging foresight activities at lower levels in the R & D system. It is clear from the case of Japan that the forecasting undertaken by MITI and STA benefits considerably from the existence of more detailed forecasts commissioned individually by firms or collectively by industrial associations. To stimulate such lower-level forecasting may initially require the provision of incentives (financial or otherwise), but ultimately British firms would surely come to appreciate like their Japanese counterparts the benefits of systematic longer-term forecasting, and would therefore elect to give such activities greater emphasis. Similarly, ministries and research-funding agencies would not only need to be involved in macro-level forecasting, but should also be encouraged to carry out more specific foresight activities relevant to their own research responsibilities.

We are fully aware that some may argue that the proposals advocated here involve a centralised approach to research planning incompatible with a British tradition of liberal pluralism. Others may contend that the Japanese approach to foresight activities depends upon highly specific features of their society and political culture. In our view, both these potential criticisms are misplaced. As regards the first, we would again re-emphasise that Japanese foresight activities depend upon the adoption of a 'bottom-up' approach, and do not require the acceptance of a high degree of centralised direction. As for the second, we would merely point out that, when the initial STA forecast was carried out at the beginning of the 1970s, relatively little interest in the long-term technological future was to be found in Japanese industry. It was the success of this and subsequent forecasts that played a part in convincing firms of the need to carry out their own, more specific forecasts which (as we saw in Chapter 6) have in turn helped improve the macro-level forecasts. There is in our view no reason why firms in Britain cannot be similarly 'won over'. Furthermore, with basic research becoming increasingly important to industry, the fact that much of this is funded and carried out within the public sector means that industry and government must of necessity learn to work more closely together in the future to ensure that research priorities are in accord with the technological needs of new science-based industries.

In conclusion, it is clear from the results of this study that the period between now and the end of the century will witness major changes in the structure of advanced nations' economies as new industries emerge and other, more mature ones are transformed by new technologies. Those new technologies will draw increasingly upon strategic research, and in turn upon areas currently seen as curiosity-orientated in nature. It was the recognition of this, together with a feeling that too many of the industrial and economic benefits derived from British contributions to basic research over past years have subsequently been appropriated by other countries, which formed the background to the commissioning of the study on which this book is based. Hopefully, its publication will play some part in stimulating wider debate on these vital issues. While there are no ready answers, a more co-ordinated approach by government and industry towards strategic research is clearly necessary if Britain is to begin exploiting more effectively the undoubted excellence of its basic science. Moreover, even though this final chapter has focused on the options for Britain, we believe our suggestions for a more systematic approach for picking future scientific winners are not without relevance to policy-makers in other industrialised countries who are currently facing very similar problems.

Notes

1. The situation in Britain has perhaps begun to improve in 1984 with the publication of an *Annual Review of Government Funded R & D* (Cabinet Office, 1984). However, its utility has been severely restricted by the limited availability of statistics from the government departments and agencies responsible for monitoring, funding and carrying out R & D.
2. A study funded by the Department of Education and Science to produce internationally comparable data on the inputs to basic academic research in Britain, France, Japan, the Netherlands, the United States and West Germany began at the Science Policy Research Unit in the latter part of 1984.

References

Cabinet Office (1984), *Annual Review of Government Funded R & D 1983*, London, HMSO.

Irvine, J., Martin, B. R. and Oldham, C. H. G. (1983), *Research Evaluation in British Science: A SPRU Review*, report to the French Ministry of Industry and Research, mimeo, Brighton, Science Policy Research Unit.

Ronayne, J. (1984), *Science in Government*, London, Edward Arnold.

STA (1972), *Science and Technology Developments up to A.D.2000*, Science and Technology Agency, Tokyo, Japan Techno-Economics Society.

The Wall Street Journal (1984), 'European panel executives acknowledge they are lagging badly in technology revolution', *The Wall Street Journal*, 31 January, p. 1 and pp. 16–17.

Index